COMMITMENTS

Published by Time and Thought Publishing House,
Washington D.C

First published under the title "Burned" in late 2013,
"Commitments" is available from book retail outlets and on line,
both in print format and in e-book format
for all popular e-readers and tablets.

For further information and details about ordering copies, contact:

Clifford Brody, at: author@cliffordbrody.com

or

Time and Thought Publishing House at media@ttphouse.com

Print edition ISBN
978-0615-9960-35

Printed in the United States of America

TTP
TIME AND THOUGHT
PUBLISHING HOUSE

Commitments

Why most of us keep on making them and breaking them…

(…when others know how to make them last!)

COMMITMENTS

To you, the reader,
and to the people about whom
you most deeply care

COMMITMENTS

Commitments

Table of Contents

COMMITMENTS

COMMITMENTS

Preface and Acknowledgements

I have a chip on my shoulder, which I will acknowledge in short order.

But my first acknowledgement is to a Beautiful Woman whose name I never learned because her conversation with us ended so abruptly.

She was bemoaning the bitter outcome to a relationship just-ended, and especially why it had failed. You see, she explained, her shallow ex-boyfriend had just walked away from their years of living together because, like all men, he was hopelessly incapable of making a long-term commitment to any woman.

"All men?" I asked, eyebrows raised.

"Yes. You're a man, so you'll never understand what making a commitment is all about," she threw back at me with no small degree of anger. And then she turned and stalked off.

Since our conversation ended right then and there, debating my gender and what that meant about my making commitments was not an option, at least not then. But Beautiful Woman's retort did have me wondering for a long time thereafter: why do people make commitments?

And not just that, either. Why are we so eager and willing to believe in commitments? Worse still, why do we go ahead and make *more* commitments, even commitments to ourselves, when the very people whom we once trusted to live up to them (including ourselves!) instead break commitments all the time and cause so much pain?

For more than a year, these questions kept on popping into my head. The more they did, the more frustrating they became. So much so, in fact, that one day I decided that the time had come to go find the answers.

Assuming there were hundreds of books about this, off to Google I went. Nothing. Bing? Ditto. Amazon? Barnes & Noble? Zip. Area libraries? No different. So, it was back to the Internet, this time using more obscure search terms in the hope that I might find my way to better answers.

No luck. The best I could come up with were a few paragraphs here and there supposedly defining the word *commitment*. One definition of *commitment* even used *commitment* to define *commitment*! Talk about going around in circles!

The only way out? Ask other people what they thought. It was good that I did, too. Their recommendations for exploring the true meaning of this common word were critical in guiding me towards using history, racial discrimination, laundry detergent, rock music, terrifying films, Broadway shows, flashlight batteries, the Olympics, ice cream, World War II, computer scientists, and a few other seemingly unrelated topics to dissect *commitment* and show what this important word really stands for.

In no way do my selections make up an exhaustive inventory of history, thought, philosophy, creativity or human habit as they relate to commitments or anything else. What you will read here is simply what I believe, underscored by my total faith in the notion that because we inevitably learn a lot from good things and bad that happen to us, we are way ahead of the game by using those lessons learned to make better-informed choices going forward.

Whatever else this book is, it is also a story of teamwork. Like cakes and pies, there are lots of different sizes, flavors, decorations and core ingredients that go into teamwork...and therefore into commitments. In learning how much teamwork is involved in making and keeping a commitment, you will come away smarter about how to make important commitments last for as long as they were meant to...even a lifetime.

Three personal biases underlie my approach to the subject of commitments:

- Bias #1: Commitments require action, not just promises, thoughts or words. They center on trust in who is going to do what and how it will get done.

- Bias #2: We are emotionally impelled to make commitments because we want other people in our lives.

- Bias #3: "Simple" is not the same as "easy", not by a long shot. Commitments are usually simple in their structure, but they are almost always hard to meet in full.

Actually, there is a fourth bias: that big chip on my shoulder I talked about at the beginning. I will acknowledge it right here and now.

My fourth bias is a firm belief that there is a lot that can and should change in the approach that therapists usually take in their counselling, and that this bears centrally on understanding what commitments are and why we make them. Therapists should be more purposeful in looking hard and *in great detail* for the positive in what makes a given person tick, rather than entering the fray with the certainty that patients have to make many changes, and big ones, if their daily lives are to improve.

Unhappily, few therapists ever spend serious time probing deeply for the elements of these positives, no less accentuating them.[1]

Worse still, this unhappy shortfall exponentially carries over—and does great harm—every time "self-help" preachers ring the same bell, which they always do: you can achieve supreme health or happiness but *only* if you agree to stop making all the mistakes you *are* making, and to change your behavior in major ways.

It doesn't take much effort to conjure up a real-life image of all those self-help, career guidance, diet guides, etiquette manuals and relationship instruction books that fill library, bookstore, online bookseller, and even supermarket checkout shelves! Or the web blogs each offering up the magic elixir for living happily ever after.

Every last one of them attempts to set itself up as *the* go-to guide. And don't they each send a seductive message! All you have to do is change this, that, or the other thing, take two pills before going to sleep tonight, and paradise will be at your doorstep tomorrow morning.

I challenge that. So does this book. The words you will read here are intended to take you in an entirely different direction, namely towards a clear understanding of the value in what you are already doing very well, namely the quality of your *Behavioral Delivery* and how this bears on making commitments.

I do not discuss Behavioral Delivery in the chapters that follow, although I do include an Appendix for those of you who would like to know more. Instead, everything from the Prologue to the last chapter will center on commitments: what they are, why we make them, why it hurts so much when they fail, and why we rely on the very same process (and are smart to do so!) even after the hurt.

What is left to do here is to deliver on my commitment to acknowledge the many people who generously gave of their time, thought, and talent to make this book much more worth your time than it otherwise would have been.

My list begins with a couple, now divorced, who allowed me to depict their unhappy ending as long as I changed their names and the city where they still live. You will meet them soon enough.

The thank-you list is much longer. It includes the very wise people, whose names we can never really know, skilled at putting information onto the Internet in ways that allow the rest of us to understand more things, ask better questions, move past intellectual roadblocks, and treat with a dose of skepticism the first answer that they render and instead dig a little deeper.

For example, you will see references in these pages to Wikipedia, to which I contribute a few dollars each year, a practice I encourage you follow as well. For all of its mostly self-acknowledged shortcomings, Wikipedia is very good at serving as a launch pad for people like me and you to find out more, to better refine our search terms, and to round out our knowledge by moving beyond the Wikipedia page to those so-often-very-useful external links that most Wikipedia pages offer up.

Then there is QuoteGarden.com, Brainyquotes.com, and Goodreads.com, from which I've been able to discover wise words offered up by *very* wise people. Hopefully, you will like how they're used here.

My deepest thanks and heartfelt acknowledgements are reserved for people whose friendship, help with this undertaking, and thoughtfulness I will always treasure.

To Jane Diefenbach, Angela Maria Nardolillo, Lisa Millora, Alina Alvarez-Ferrer, Ridley Williams, Frank Guzzardo, Nina Armah, and Joshua Copeland, all co-frequenters with me at Tryst, an amazing Washington, D.C. coffee house: how patient you were in hearing out what I wanted to do, and how great it was to have your encouragement. I am so indebted to you, and happily so; thank you.

To Linda Noel who teaches American History at Morgan State University in Baltimore and manages also to get great things done pounding away at her laptop while at Tryst, I am especially indebted for putting me on to my editor, John Sprovieri in Chicago. It was John who helped transform my miles-long sentences and paragraphs into a much more easily-digestible meal, and who wisely counseled me to tone done excesses so that any message I wanted to share could make its way to the surface.

To Rebecca Sheir and Kavitha Cardoza, a remarkable team of producer-reporters at Washington D.C.'s public radio station WAMU, I can only wish someday to come close to meeting the high standards you have set in translating your awesome inspiration, creativity and perseverance into words and sounds that daily capture the imagination of the station's hundreds of thousands of listeners and supporters not only here in the mid-Atlantic states but also world-wide through the Internet and the National Public Radio network. As much as you two have inspired me—and you have!—to dig deeper and uncover better words to convey key thoughts in this book, I will never come close to matching what you bring to the table every single day. Wow!

To Lisa Priebe, thank you Big Time for your willingness to take on the arduous task of looking carefully at the order of my thinking and the wording of key elements in this book, your extraordinary capacity to hone in fast on what it was that I was really trying to say, to recommend better ways to get those points across, and your light-speed in delivering those solutions. You are so good at what you do!

To the Fieschi family in France—Pascal and Aude, and their now-grown children Ariane, Claire, Barbara, Dorothée and Pierre Emmanuel—I owe special thanks for an extraordinary friendship that has lasted more than forty years.

Separately and together, these seven remarkable people of *"la famille Fieschi"* (the Fieschi family) have allowed me a rare, treasured glimpse into the dynamics of a shared commitment—to enrich their familial ties—that has survived just about every tough challenge that life can possibly offer up.

More than that, their commitment to one another not only has thrived but also grown as each of these distinctly creative individuals charted radically different courses in their lives.

Their formula for success? Finding the right elements in their separate and unique selves to build ever-stronger ties of love and respect for one another that today powerfully bind them together.

If the Fieschis could bottle their magic formula for family and commitment, the rest of us for sure would be lining up to buy their tonic by the truckload.

COMMITMENTS

Prologue

Ever see *Promises, Promises?*

A Grammy-award-winning Broadway musical that ran for 1,281 performances from 1968 to 1972, this Burt Bacharach-Neil Simon-Hal David masterpiece gave rise to two great Dionne Warwick hits, "Promises, Promises," and "I'll Never Fall in Love Again."

As entertaining as it was, *Promises, Promises* also had a serious side. Set in the highly charged corporate world of New York City in the late 1960s, *Promises, Promises* was a tragicomic tale of broken promises unfolding between husbands, wives and lovers.

The show's farcical encounters between people in love and married people with lovers offered up an image of the way things are that can easily be traced back to the way things were between husbands and wives centuries before the musical's Broadway premier on December 1, 1968.

The musical rang true in 1968—and again for audiences seeing the terrific 2011 Broadway revival—because it told a story as ageless as humanity: after people fail abjectly to do what they committed to do, they continue to make and break commitments again and again...and again!

1968 Broadway cast of Promises, Promises, including lead player
Jerry Orbach (bowler hat), later of "Law & Order" fame

Why do they do it? And, for that matter, what is the meaning of commitment? Is it the same thing as a promise? A vow? An oath? Should we look upon them all as the same?

Linguists and etymologists might argue that all these words do mean the same thing.

Well, they don't.

Understanding how these words differ—and why commitment is in a league by itself—is the key to learning from history rather than just repeating it. It also points to the secret sauce for making the right commitments at the right time, demanding the same of others, and making sure those commitments stick.

In this book, I often focus on marriages as one good way to figure out what commitments are, what they're not, and why they work—or don't. Although the history of marriages that lasted, and the sometimes sordid histories of marriages that did not, tell us a good deal about commitments, they do not come close to telling us everything we need to know. Yet. there is evidence that no matter when or where or for what reason commitments are made, they are all the same. Successful commitments all work out for the same basic reasons. And, unsuccessful commitments all fail for the same basic reasons.

Wouldn't life be easier if all successful commitments shared just one secret sauce, so we could simply stir in the right amount to the ones we make and then live happily ever after?

Let's find out if they do.

COMMITMENTS

1. A Tale of Two Commitments

"Please," she cried over the phone. "I need the abortion! I can't have a child now. If the father doesn't approve, I can't get it done here."

"But I'm *not* the father!"

******

We were meeting for the first time. He extended his hand to shake mine. I looked him in the eye, dumbfounded by how much I despised him. He shifted uncomfortably, looking away, looking downward.

At which point I simply turned and walked away, never looking back, without the slightest regret, not then, not now, at refusing to lift my hand to meet his.

We had been married, K and I, for seven years, tying the knot right out of college. Back then, I was a newly minted U.S. diplomat, so damned sure I actually would help achieve world peace that it didn't matter — well, at least not too much — that I was also facing a two-year obligatory stint in the Army.

"Don't think twice about it, Cliff," people at the State Department had said, so sure they would persuade the Pentagon to give up on sending me to Vietnam and instead let me serve out my Army ROTC commission at the State Department itself. Predicted these ever-so-smug diplomatic colleagues of mine: "How could they not?"

How could they not? Very easily, that's how. The Defense Department never lets go whenever it can beat the State Department in battles big and small—which is just about always, by the way.

So off to the Army I went in my fatigues, first as a greenhorn lieutenant supervising grim solders off-loading body bags, each with a very dead U.S. soldier inside, that had been unceremoniously shipped back in soulless, non-descript steel-grey freighters from Vietnam to the Oakland Marine Terminal across the Bay from San Francisco.

And in less than a year, it was my turn: on a chartered DC-9 to Vietnam for an obligatory year on the ground there, not that far north of the relative safety of Saigon but still dodging bullets, all while B-52s dropped their lethal calling cards…for what purpose, Dear God? For What Purpose?

By late 1968, having survived Vietnam, I could at last continue on with my State Department Foreign Service appointment. After a half-year in Washington learning French, off I went to pass the next two years in France as a wet-behind-the-ears "glorified gopher" at the U.S. Embassy in Paris.

None of my experiences, either in Vietnam or France, could have prepared me for that cold and drizzly morning back in Washington early in 1972, when I found myself on a dismal street corner hopelessly in the dark about a frenzied night of sex. Not my night. Hers. My wife K's. With someone else.

She had literally walked out the door months before, casually explaining that she had met a "someone else" and just couldn't stay away from him anymore. And now? I had to look her and Someone Else in the eye *and* save them both.

Rue Gozlin, all of one-block-long, a street of happier times where we lived in Paris, before K met her "someone else".

"Please, Cliff," she had cried over the phone. "I need the abortion! I can't have a child now. If the father doesn't approve, I can't get it done here."

COMMITMENTS

"But I'm *not* the father!"

"I know!" she burst out. "But we're not divorced yet, so you *are* the father whether you are or not. I can't go in there now and say he's the father. He won't admit it anyway. And they won't let me have the abortion unless the father agrees. And anyway, *you're* the father because that's what I already wrote down."

"So I have to take the rap and bail you out—and him, too?" I'm screaming now.

Not her, though. Just silence. Then, finally a whispered "Yes."

I could easily have said no and thrown in a few more choice words for good measure. Instead, "Okay. When and where?"

So it came to pass on that tombstone-grey spring morning that K emerged from the doorway of a nondescript building in southwest Washington D.C., paper and pen in hand. She was frightened. I signed. And that's when Someone Else came walking down the street towards us, a weak smile on his face, extending his hand in greeting.

What was the commitment that made me put that pen to paper? What was my failed commitment, and to whom had I made it, that to this day has me regretting that I didn't tell him exactly where he could shove his hand?

COMMITMENTS

Last summer's song is making a comeback on the radio,
and on the highway overpass,
the only metaphysical vandal in America has written
MEMORY LOVES TIME
in big black spraypaint letters
which makes us wonder if Time loves Memory back.

Last night I dreamed of X again
She's like a stain on my subconscious sheets.
Years ago she penetrated me
but though I scrubbed and scrubbed and scrubbed,
I never got her out,
but now I'm glad.

What I thought was an end turned out to be a middle.
What I thought was a brick wall turned out to be a tunnel.
What I thought was an injustice
turned out to be a color of the sky.

> from *"A Color of the Sky"* by Tony Hoagland from
> *What Narcissism Means To Me.* © Graywolf Press, 2003,
> with permission from the author.

On Monday, January 10, 2000...

...just ten days after the new millennium began, CNN interrupted normal programming at 5:26 P.M. eastern time to broadcast breaking news of a surprise corporate merger:

> "In a stunning development, America Online Inc. announced plans to acquire Time Warner Inc. for roughly $182 billion in stock and debt...creating a digital media powerhouse [valued at $350 billion] with the potential to reach every American in one form or another.
>
> "With dominating positions in the music, publishing, news, entertainment, cable and Internet industries, the combined company, called AOL Time Warner, will boast unrivaled assets among other media and online companies."[2]

On that very same day, in Keokuk, Iowa, there was another marriage, that of 24-year-old Mary Marides to her beau, 25-year-old Robert Stephson. Having known each other since childhood, the young sweethearts dated in high school and became a real hometown "item" after Robbie returned to Iowa from a five-year Army stint.

"Their marriage ceremony was beautiful," said Pastor Jim Haverford of the Presbyterian Church, quoted in the *Daily Gate City*, Keokuk's hometown newspaper. "If ever there is a couple whose marriage will last a lifetime, it's theirs," the beaming clergyman added.

Fast forward almost ten years.

On December 9, 2009, only two months shy of their merger's ten-year anniversary, Time Warner and AOL divorced. A few days later on the actual 10-year anniversary of this once "digital media powerhouse" merger, the *New York Times* observed grimly that:

> "A decade ago, America Online merged with Time Warner in a deal valued at a stunning $350 billion. It was then, and is now, the largest merger in American business history.
>
> "The trail of despair in subsequent years included countless job losses, the decimation of retirement accounts, investigations by the Securities and Exchange Commission and the Justice Department, and countless executive upheavals....
>
> "To call the transaction the worst in history, as it is now taught in business schools, does not begin to tell the story of how some of the brightest minds in technology and media collaborated to produce a deal now regarded by many as a colossal mistake."[3]

That's not all. On the very same day that Time Warner and AOL broke up, Keokuk's Family Court finalized Robbie and Mary's divorce.

What happened?

On that fateful December day in 2009, each set of partners conceded not that their Year 2000 commitments to one another had ended but instead that those commitments had actually failed.

This difference—between ending a commitment and a commitment that fails—is as wide and deep as the Grand Canyon. It explains why we make commitments in the first place and why we then break most of them. It explains why, when we're aware that future commitments are likely to fail or be broken, too, that we still go back and make them again and again. And, it explains why this is absolutely the right thing for us to do.

Is it possible that the AOL-Time Warner merger and the Stephsons' marriage represented identical commitments? Is it possible that those commitments also failed for the same reasons?

Absolutely yes! It wouldn't surprise me, though, if at first you disagreed. After all, AOL and Time Warner as companies, not people, were nothing at all like Robert and Mary. The two corporate giants owned quality brands, employed thousands of people, managed worldwide media empires out of massive headquarters buildings in Virginia and New York City, deployed legions of marketers, lawyers, accountants, web sites, and IT specialists to make things go smoothly, and, before their marriage, had already earned stellar reputations for delivering leading edge consumer, media and technology services.

By contrast, there was nothing corporate about Mary and Robert. They were simply two people in love who committed to share their lives together, build a family, pay off the mortgage, and live out their lives in the town they loved until death did them part.

And yet, despite all these differences, AOL and Time Warner's commitments to each other were exactly the same as Mary and Robert's. Consider these facts:

- Fact #1: Both sets of partners entered into a formal relationship with one another where each party knew that the other was counting on them for the future success of the marriage.

- Fact #2: Each partner explicitly confirmed to the other that they were agreeing to common goals in their respective marriages.

- Fact #3: Each had agreed to work hard together to achieve those common goals.

- Fact #4: Each also agreed to do specific things, and avoid doing other things, to make sure that the marriage would work.

- Fact #5: Each expected that there would be offspring after the marriage was consummated (subsidiaries in the case of AOL-Time Warner, and children in the case of Robert and Mary).

– Fact #6: Each partner knew that the future welfare of these offspring would depend entirely on how each "parent" met shared responsibilities to assure their offspring stayed healthy, grew and prospered.

– Fact #7: Each knew that real money, and potentially lots of it, would be at stake, and that the idea was to earn more of it over time so that everyone would be better off.

– Fact #8, and the most important fact of all: each partner was led to believe by the other that their expectations of one another to do all of these things (and much, much more) were totally realistic, and that their partners could be counted on 100 percent to deliver the goods.

Despite all of these identical attributes, and despite all the micro-commitments each partner elected to make to the other every day after their wedding ceremonies, both unions came to an end not just because certain commitments to one another merely *ended* but also because those commitments actually *failed*—something else that Time Warner, AOL and the Stephsons all had in common.

How and why this happened will help to explain what commitments are, why we make them, why they fail, and—despite the awful pain we feel when they do fail—why we willingly do it all over again to get what we want.

COMMITMENTS

2. Promises, Vows, Oaths, and Commitments: Aren't They All the Same?

Had she seduced me with the gracefulness of her smile and her skills at dressage...had she beguiled me just as she had that enormous stallion into such willing obedience?

******

She could have been a champion rider. Maybe she will be someday. She had achievement, reputation, and medals. She bubbled over with pride. She excited everyone around her with her big beautiful smile and sensuality. And she had energy that wouldn't stop. My God, you could touch it!

It was painfully clear, though, that her day in, day out scrambling for the next dollar was sapping her of any immunity to sudden, devastating injury to her soul, her profession and even her physical self. Jumping horses with no health insurance? Lord of Lords!

"All we need is some money and then we can do it! Help us! You'll see!"

Why didn't I see? What was it about all the writing, all the planning, all the pressure that failed to tell us where all her earlier money had gone? How could she make the case—or worse, how could I make the case—that new backers would see their money well-spent, that maybe, just maybe, they were betting on a winner?

The power of the person and the power of the steed, as one.

She was a star. She was going to bring glamour and glory to the rest of us, there, in the ring, with a finesse rooted in childhood, shaped in her teens, and then in her early 20s, honed by the most eminent equestrians in Europe. Watching her direct that beautiful stallion to dance in the ring and clear all the jumps seemingly by magic, I found it easy to believe in her claim: she was *certain* to make it to the U.S. Equestrian Team and compete in the next Olympics. It was so obvious to her. Couldn't the rest of us all just see it? Feel it?

I certainly did. And so it became my self-appointed job to persuade wealthy donors to join in and sponsor her dream of Olympic glory. The more I wrote (the inevitably turgid investment documents that accompany capital raises), the more she left me alone to prepare not just a vision, but all the other information that the lawyers, accountants and investors had to see before even one dollar would pass into her hands. Alas, the more time I spent at the keyboard, the more I sensed I was going further and further out on a limb. Had she seduced me with the gracefulness of her smile and her skills at dressage and eventing?[4]   Had she beguiled me just as she that enormous stallion into such willing obedience?

I spent months tediously writing and rewriting, straining under the weight of complicated legalistic words, pages, chapters. How your investment will be protected. How your money will be at risk. How your dollars will be spent. How you can count on her to deliver. I spent months more just on the financial modeling—thousands of numbers in tortured spreadsheets.

"We'll get you the stuff, Cliff, I promise," she and her trainers assured me. "Whatever information they need, we'll get it to you for sure. But we need the money now."

It never came. Neither her information, nor my money or anyone else's.

How could I have been duped into committing so much time, so much of my reputation, so much midnight oil, to solving her problem?

Turns out, she hadn't fooled me. I fooled myself. I should've known better. Why didn't I? How did I fail this commitment to myself?

Oaths are but words, and words but wind.
Samuel Butler

Not the maker of plans and promises, but rather the one who offers faithful service in small matters. This is the person who is most likely to achieve what is good and lasting.
Johann Wolfgang von Goethe

It is an immutable law in business that words are words, explanations are explanations, promises are promises but only performance is reality.
Harold Geneen

Throughout this book...

...I am sharing a few of my own life stories, as well as other real-life examples, that hopefully will make it easier for you to understand what commitments are, what they aren't, and why they are so different from promises, vows, oaths, or pledges.

Once we pin down what commitments are, we can more easily uncover why we make them, why so many of them fail—especially the most important ones—and why we make more commitments even when we're so badly burned by the ones that didn't work. And why we should!

So, you may ask, what *is* a commitment? Isn't it the same as a *promise*, *vow*, or *oath*? What do dictionaries tell us about these words? Well, as they used to say in Brooklyn, New York where I was born: "Yer pays yer money and takes yer choice!"

Consult the Merriam-Webster online dictionary and you will discover that a *promise* is "a declaration that one will do or refrain from doing something specified or a legally binding declaration that gives the person to whom it is made a right to expect or to claim the performance or forbearance of a specified act."

Whew! That is some tortured language, don't you think? Maybe we can do better.

Wikipedia says that a *promise* is:

> "...a commitment by someone to do or not do something. As a noun, 'promise' means a declaration assuring that one will or will not do something. As a verb it means to commit oneself by a promise to do or give."

Now isn't that interesting? Wikipedia's definition is not only easier to understand, but it also sneaks in the idea of commitment! Maybe we need to go back to the first dictionary and look up *commitment*.

Our online standby Merriam-Webster defines commitment two ways. The first is the action of putting someone in a hospital, treatment facility or prison, a definition we won't bother with here (except perhaps when my friends insist: "Brody, you're crazy!").

What fits better for our purposes is the follow-on Merriam-Webster offering:

> "...an agreement or pledge to do something in the future; especially: an engagement to assume a financial obligation at a future date, [or] something pledged [or] the state or an instance of being obligated or emotionally impelled [such as] a commitment to a cause."

Now we're getting somewhere, especially with those thoughts about the future, and about being "obligated or emotionally impelled." Tuck "future" and "impelled" in the back of your mind for now—we'll come back to them later on—while we move back to Wikipedia, which offers this about commitment:

- Promise, or personal commitment. (A bit circular, using commitment to define commitment!)

- Contract, a legally binding exchange of promises.

- Brand commitment. (The only shampoo I will ever buy is...)

- Involuntary commitment, the use of legal means ... to commit a person to a mental hospital ... or psychiatric ward. (They're after me again!)

- Ontological commitment, belief in an ontology in philosophy. (Ontology is the philosophic study of the nature of being...way over my head!)

– Organizational commitment. (These guys don't quit, do they, again using commitment to define commitment!)

– Commitment scheme, in cryptography. (Ask the CIA what this means!)

– Commit (data management) to make changes permanent in data management. (Geeky.)

– Kingsbury Commitment, the beginning of AT&T's monopoly in the telephone industry. (Who knew?)

– Climate commitment, a model of climate change. (Going around in circles again, or maybe we're just being cyclonic.)

– Commitment (Seal album).

– Commitment (Lucky Boys "Confusion" album).

– Commitment, the 1998 LeAnn Rimes hit song.

Pay dirt at last! Check out that LeAnn Rimes song; it is great! Otherwise, we can't rely too much on this Wikipedia list. Too many of these items actually trap us in a dizzying cycle of circular logic that we need to escape.

And we can!

COMMITMENTS

3. Commitments and What Religion Tells Us...or Not!

Sitting in her decrepit old office in that decrepit old building...I couldn't believe my ears as she feigned sympathy and explained that the "B" was no mistake.

"Huh? How's that?" I asked.

"Well, you're a Jew," she replied. "You can't ever understand Jesus the right way. The best you can get is a 'B.' "

******

Professor Bonney was a nun. Actually, she was an ex-nun, which surprised me since I hadn't known until then that someone who had been married to God could go on to divorce Him.

In retrospect, I can see now that it wasn't the only thing I didn't know. I was the only Jewish kid in a one-semester course on "The Life and Teachings of Jesus" at this small Methodist college. I had assumed that my God-fearing Christian classmates would certainly be keener than me to look better in the eyes of the Lord and hence take the professor's words more seriously than I would. What the hell, all I wanted was an easy course to get through first semester senior year doing the least work possible.

Surprise! Once I got into it, I became thrilled with the knowledge that Professor Bonney was sharing. I thought a great deal of the good professor, absorbed every word of the arduous reading assignments she meted out, and became totally fascinated by the ins and outs of religious scholarship. Sucking up all those tiny printed annotations in the margins of our text, I found it both easy and compelling to navigate the maze of coursework that most all of the others in the room thought ever so tortured.

Imagine! Me, Jewish, really getting into how one gospel differed from another! Why didn't Matthew, Mark, Luke and John see the life of Jesus identically? What were the roots of all the other inconsistencies spread out in the apostles' written words—or the words written about them?

Denny Hall, Dickinson College, in 1940, two years before I was born...and then reborn in 1964 into the reality of what Jews could and could not do.

To find out, I became skilled with the whys and wherefores of leading players whose names never made their way into my Hebrew School curriculum, pulling A or A+ on every exam and paper I handed in. I hadn't done anywhere near as well in Hebrew School—actually, I had loathed that Wednesday afternoon prison! How cool was it now, I sat in Professor Bonney's classroom thinking, that I would soon be getting a Jesus-based "A" that would raise my GPA even higher. Who would have thought that going down this not-so-kosher road would turn out to be such a blast!

Think again, Jew Boy! When the envelope arrived over winter break with my grades, I tore it open eagerly—only to discover I got a "B" from the once-nun.

Me, a "B"? There had to be some mistake. Once I got back to campus, I just *knew* I would be able to sit down with Professor Bonney and, without a second's hesitation, she would fix the mistake. Hadn't she already told me so many times before how impressed she was with my classwork?

Think again, Jew Boy! Sitting in her decrepit old office in a decrepit old building that passed itself off as a National Historic Landmark, I couldn't believe my ears as she feigned sympathy and explained that the "B" was no mistake.

"Huh? How's that?" I asked.

"Well, you're a Jew," she replied. "You can't ever understand Jesus the right way. The best you can get is a 'B.'"

She had said what she meant and meant what she said. So did I, as my eyes sliced her into pieces with sudden anger. I spit out a nasty expletive and stalked out.

What was Professor Bonney's commitment to me? What was mine to her? What does religion tell us about all that?

There are three religious truths: 1) Jews do not recognize Jesus as the Messiah. 2) Protestants do not recognize the Pope as the leader of the Christian faith. 3) Baptists do not recognize each other in the liquor store or at Hooters.

Author Unknown (from QuoteGarden.com)

Oh, Honey, God don't care which church you go, long as you show up!

Robert Harling, Steel Magnolias

How many observe Christ's birthday! How few his precepts! O! Tis easier to keep holidays than commandments.

Benjamin Franklin, Poor Richard's Almanack, 1757

If the dictionary definition...

...of commitment won't get us very far in understanding what a commitment is, maybe religion has an answer.

To find out, let's climb aboard the wayback machine for a short trip into the history of religion. We'll start with the Ten Commandments and, to make it even easier, look at just one commandment, the Tenth:

> Thou shalt not covet thy neighbor's house, thy
> neighbor's wife, nor his servant, nor his ox, nor his
> donkey, nor anything that is thy neighbor's.

Implicit but undeniable in this commandment is confirmation that by violating these strictures, you would be breaking your own commitment to someone else, or interfering with someone else's commitment either to you or someone else.

It is obvious that God was giving Moses this Tenth Commandment (and the other nine, too) as solutions to solve problems that had been around for a long time. Indeed, people already knew very well what commitments were, what they were meant to achieve, and why they were important. Yet they were still breaking them left and right, and was God ever determined to put a stop to it!

But is the word commitment itself to be found in any of the commandments? Surprise! Not only is it missing from the Ten Commandments, it does not appear anywhere—anywhere!—in any version of the Bible (Old or New Testament), with one sole modern day poetic license exception![5]

Let's try to find some other words that people often think are equivalent to commitment. In a line of thinking accepted by many

Christians as well as Jews, the Jewish scholar Louis Jacobs argues that both *vows* and *oaths* have played central roles in people's lives over the centuries. However, in his benchmark study *The Jewish Religion: A Companion,*[6] Jacobs notes that a vow is quite different from an oath.

The core distinction between oaths and vows, Jacobs tells us, is found in Numbers 30:3: "When a man voweth a vow unto the Lord, or sweareth an oath to bind his soul with a bond, he shall not break his word; he shall do according to all that proceedeth out of his mouth."

This verse has come to be interpreted by many religious scholars, both Christian and Jewish, to mean that an oath refers to enlisting God as witness. For example, you will do "this" with "that," and you are asking God to be witness to your making the deal. On the other hand, a vow is a deal made directly with God to do something, whether with a tangible thing (avoid high-cholesterol foods, pick up the brush and go paint the garage) or intangible (swear off cursing).

Splitting hairs? Maybe so. And maybe not. These two definitions clearly point to two separate roles for God: one as partner in the deal (vow) and the other as witness to the deal (oath). Partner vs. witness: whether it is God or anyone else, this distinction is critical in understanding vows and oaths. As for commitments? The word is still missing!

Other scholars of Jewish history argue that making vows in fact is foolish, since people are bound to break them, whether for good reason or bad. In fact, the most holy of Jewish High Holy Days, Yom Kippur, recognizes this by providing the opportunity for nullifying vows taken unwittingly or foolishly, including those made out of spite, jealousy or anger.

Why? I may vow never to drive above the speed limit or to run a stop sign. The day came, though, when my seven-year-old daughter was stung by a bee the first time, leaving her face swelling bright red and her body convulsing as she gasped for every breath. You can bet that I drove much faster than the speed limit and blew past a great many stop signs to get her to the emergency room—and fast! So much for my vow.

Still nothing about commitments!

What does Islam have to say? Over the centuries, Islamic scholars have gone to great lengths to clarify that, on the one hand, a person making a promise must keep it or be considered a sinner (a "hypocrite"). On the other, Islam is equally clear that there are circumstances when a person may fail to keep a promise yet not sin.

This reasoning is anchored in practicality: a person may forget to keep a promise, may be forced to act against a promise, or may be prevented from fulfilling a promise (say, by a snowstorm, the electricity going out, or a flat tire). In no sense does Islam offer a "Get Out of Jail Free" card to be used at will to free oneself from a promise. However, it nonetheless recognizes that there are indeed times when a promise may go by the board for very good reason.

Still nothing about commitments! Maybe vows and oaths and promises and commitments are all really the same thing, with that pesky word "commitment" simply a modern day term. Well, let's see...

Many Christians historically have made a distinction between promises and oaths or vows. Much like in Judaism, an oath, they believe, is a promise invoking God as a witness, while a vow is a solemn promise to God that binds the person to meet a moral good.

The Catholic sacrament of confession and equivalent practices among other Christian faiths to ask for God's understanding and forgiveness bespeaks awareness that whether we call them vows, oaths, or promises, Christians of all persuasions break them all the time and need a way back. Yet there is still nothing specific about commitments to be found.

Buddhism addresses the concept in a "sort-of" way. Although there appear to be no explicit definitions of promise, oath, vow or commitment in Buddhist thought, the religion's Fourth Precept states: "I undertake to...abstain from false speech." One could argue that taking an oath or vow with no intention of keeping it is a concrete violation of that precept.

Likewise in Hinduism, itself a very sophisticated system of belief and conduct evolving over the millennia, there is no single way of viewing oaths, vows or promises, no less commitments. In his essay on Hindu ethics, Swami Nikhilananda Ramakrishna at the Vivekananda Center in New York City writes:

> "Ethics, which concerns itself with the study of conduct, is derived, in Hinduism, from certain spiritual concepts; it forms the steel-frame foundation of the spiritual life...

> "Hindu ethics differs from modern scientific ethics, which is largely influenced by biology; for according to this latter, whatever is conducive to the continuous survival of a particular individual or species is good for it...

> "[Hindu ethics] also differ from utilitarian ethics, whose purpose is to secure the maximum utility for a society by eliminating friction and guaranteeing for its members a harmonious existence. Hindu ethics prescribes the disciplines for a spiritual life, which are to be observed consciously or unconsciously as long as man lives...

Within this framework, it can safely be assumed that Hindus historically have been and today are obligated to honor all vows, oaths, or promises made. Yet at the same time, Hindus are left to their own devices to follow the norms, meaning and penalties that society, not religion, applies to taking a vow or oath, or making a promise and then breaking it. In no sense has God handed down a neat, clean, explicit "Hindu" definition for any of these three words, nor for commitment, either.

What are we to conclude from all this? Or from the conclusion that no religion seems to define the actual word commitment while explicitly defining vow and oath?

For one, that there is no single definition rooted in the world's religions that neatly distinguishes commitments, vows, oaths or promises from one another, or even defines them the same way as synonyms meaning the same thing.

Rather, from the religious history point of view, it is much the same situation as when Supreme Court Justice Potter Stewart wrote in his opinion in the benchmark 1964 Jacobellis v. Ohio decision on obscenity: "...hard-core pornography is hard to define, but I know it when I see it..."

If it is also true, even without a universally agreed definition for commitment, that you know a commitment when you see it, then it matters little whether you may have trouble finding in religion a quintessentially perfect definition for commitment, vow, oath or promise.

The key is that all of us may really know it when we see it or hear it. Or so we think.

COMMITMENTS

4. Commitments and Six Royal Wives

"L...," I said softly, "ask them to clarify what they mean." She did, and they simply repeated what they had so casually said the first time around: can I steal the goods for them?

Takes but an instant: "Go f*** yourselves," I mutter. L hears me, they don't. And her face gets even redder.

"Mr. Brody, do you want me to translate *that?*"

******

Springtime, 1993. Moscow. 12 Neglinnaya Street. Dingy and covered in soot, the unremarkable nineteenth century urban palace standing before me hardly suggested that the handful of guys inside held all the cards and power over every last ruble and dollar in Russia.

Yellowing. Fading. Decrepit. What a fitting setting for a bunch of over-age, chain-smoking, ex-Soviet banker-politicians whose careers had begun while Stalin was still in charge. Maybe the blood on their hands had been washed away to everyone else's satisfaction, but not to mine. Habits die hard: who in the last couple of years, I wondered, had they and their comrades-in-arms held in the basement dungeon, executed in the back yard, or sent off to Siberia just to hold on to their own seats of power in this new post-Soviet Russian government?

Before: Russian Central Bank, pre-1917 Russian Revolution picture postcard

After: an early 2013 snowfall. Alas, I was there during a grim 1994 "During"

Better not be too judgmental, I said to myself, at least not right now. Just suck it all up and follow through. Didn't I need something from them much more than they needed anything from me? With Citibank, Texas Instruments, Land O'Lakes, Dell Inc., AT&T and a few other major corporations all riding on my coattails and my Russia network, today's goal was to get the final decision on a business deal from the powers-that-be inside this vainglorious Russian Central Bank. Better that I leave moral judgments for another day and someone else's dollar.

L walked in front of me as a young guard in ill-fitting gray-green garb led us up the grand staircase. Huh? As many times as I'd been in this old dump, we had always been taken over to the rickety side elevators, up to one or another nondescript office where Lenin's and Stalin's photos surely had once hung on the now starkly unadorned walls.

Not today.

"What's up?" I asked her. L didn't know. We dutifully trailed like puppy dogs behind our minion until we arrived at two ornately carved wooden doors that opened onto the largest space I'd ever seen in this once city mansion. It was not quite the ballroom-sized Federal Reserve boardroom in Washington, but it was not bad at all for a central bank. An elegantly long conference table stretched all the way to the other end of the room, with the ubiquitous desk parked at the top end as only the Russians can do it. It was way down at that other end where we were finally seated.

"C'mon, L…. What gives?" I again asked her.

"I really don't know."

Maybe we did get the deal after all, I thought. Why else would we be here?

After a few minutes, a door opened at the other end of the room by the desk. Two grey bureaucrats officiously walked in and sat down, one at the desk itself, the other in a chair to his right. I recognized the second fellow. But L and I both knew that Mr. Unknown, seated at the desk, was running the show. The guy at the desk anywhere in Russia runs the show.

We exchanged a few formalities, L faithfully interpreting their words and mine. Then, suddenly, no more chitchat: they wanted to get down to business.

"Mr. Brody," the one at the desk began in Russian. "We so appreciate that your consortium of such illustrious companies came to Moscow to make that wonderful presentation to our experts about what they can sell to us for modernizing our banking system."

I let the faint praise fly by me.

"And you were correct," he went on, "that their integrated hardware and software solution is second to none. It is magnificent."

So polite, so erudite, this faint praise. Okay, where's the damnation, where's the bomb?

"You know," the fellow continued, "we have so many highly trained computer scientists here in Russia, and all the dollars we need to buy computers. You will understand, we believe, that it makes no sense for us to buy a whole assortment of hardware and software from foreign companies when we need so very little. The one part of your system that links all the banks together so effectively, well, we don't have that and also know it would take us years to build it ourselves. We'll pay you handsomely if you could just procure that for us. Can you? We simply don't need any of the rest. And we don't want it."

Perhaps, I thought, they had missed a key point we had made many months earlier when about a hundred of us slogged our way in the dead of Moscow winter to strut our stuff. It had taken us more than a year to handcraft a complete package just for Russia. Every component was tailored by each company in the consortium to fit and work perfectly with the others. Where did that selling point get lost, I asked myself?

So I make the pitch again, emphasizing how the Central Bank would cut years and billions of dollars from the cost of putting a working system in place simply by deploying our solution. There was no better way anywhere at any price for reining in the Wild West financial corruption that was grinding Russia's banks into mincemeat and propelling the country's triple-digit inflation rate.

"We understand all that, Mr. Brody, but if you could just steal that one software kernel and deliver it to us, we can do the rest."

L's face had turned bright red. I could not believe the words in English as she faithfully translated what the Russian had just uttered.

"What did you just say?" I whispered to her, forgetting for the moment that she really hadn't said anything on her own and was instead just the mouthpiece for someone else's message. Meanwhile, the two guys up there at the far end of the room were smiling, waiting, with hands neatly folded in front of them.

She repeated what she had just said.

Kurt Vonnegut, I'm calling out silently, help me! Russia's version of the Federal Reserve wants me to shoplift for them!

"L...," I said softly, "ask them to clarify what they mean." She did, and they simply repeated what they had so casually said the first time around: can I steal the goods for them?

Takes but an instant: "Go f*** yourselves," I mutter. L hears me, they don't. And her face gets even redder.

"Mr. Brody, do you want me to translate *that*?"

"No, L..., no. Let's try this." And what I next offered up was a fantasy string of eight-syllable words about how the magic code they wanted was so deeply melded into the rest of the software and hardware that there was no physical way for anyone to pull the heist off successfully. Even though I knew we could easily do what they wanted.

If we wanted to...

Then it dawned on me. By refusing these two thugs, I was doing more than just kissing goodbye a few hundred thousand dollars of my company's time and money. I was orchestrating my permanent exile from the very Russian government power network that took me years to build.

Just as suddenly, my fears of a cellar dungeon did not figure into the equation any more. Nor did these two guys. If the only way to play ball here is to steal things for Russia's Central Bank, I reasoned, then we would do better by unwinding all the agreements with all the other companies in the consortium and just calling the whole thing off—even if that took many more months and a lot more money.

"Too bad, Mr. Brody," our two hosts offered up as L and I walked out. "We would have loved to do business with you."

I'll bet they would!

I have not failed. I've just found 10,000 ways that won't work.

Thomas Edison

I don't know the key to success, but the key to failure is trying to please everybody.

Bill Cosby

The hardest thing to learn in life is which bridge to cross and which to burn.

David Russell

I've missed more than 9,000 shots in my career. I've lost almost 300 games. Twenty-six times I've been trusted to take the game winning shot and missed. I've failed over and over and over again in my life, and that is why I succeed.

Michael Jordan

We have now seen...

...that the world's religions have no agreed definition for commitment, and that in the end, we may just have to learn to be comfortable simply knowing a commitment when we see one.

To find out whether this is really good enough, let's adjust the dial on the wayback machine and head over to sixteenth century England. Our hosts? Henry VIII (1491 - 1547), three Catharines, two Annes, and one Jane, each Henry's wife at one time or another.

The latest in a long line of English kings, Henry VIII indeed had lots of wives, six in all, five of whom he disposed of one way or another so he could marry the next one. Two, Anne Boleyn and Catharine Howard, were beheaded. Two more, Catharine of Aragon and Anne of Cleves, he managed to divorce. And one, Jane Seymour, died shortly after childbirth.

Lucky Number Six, Catharine Parr, made it simply by outliving then-decrepit old Henry.

What's remarkable in this saga, for our purposes, is not so much that Henry got away with all this but instead the tremendous effort that the king and his advisors made to justify both his separation from each wife and his moving on to the next one.

In modern parlance, Henry could not simply walk out on one woman, get a no-fault divorce, and move on to the next wife. Quite the contrary. In his younger years, Henry VIII was a practicing Catholic, as were most of his countrymen at the time. Hence, divorce was not an option. So it was that the Good King Henry was forced by strict doctrine to go to extraordinary lengths—physical, political, and religious—to win approval from other domestic and foreign royalty and the Pope himself, before he could move on from his first wife, Catharine of Aragon, to the second, Ann Boleyn.

The challenges Henry and his coterie faced to secure Catholic Church blessings for an annulment of his first marriage were complicated by the fact that in the sixteenth century, written and verbal pleas by the King or his representatives—to anyone anywhere for anything—had to move by sail, horseback, wagon and foot. Offloading his first wife meant not only that Catholic Henry had to get a dispensation from Rome to marry Anne Boleyn, but also that he had to wait it out while his emissaries spent weeks during 1527 traveling, first to cross the English Channel and then across the European continent with Henry's plea in hand to Rome for that precious papal "yes."

Alas, the traveling band failed to secure the Pope's thumb's up. The royal entourage then took yet more weeks making its way back to London with the rather unwelcome news that all had failed, leaving Henry no choice but to wait things out while he came up with a Plan B.

And quite a wait it was! It took Henry six years to figure it all out, and then assemble the pieces into what became known as the English Reformation and the emergence of the Anglican Church. All the while, Catharine remained Henry's first wife only in name, having been unceremoniously banished from the Court in 1531 after being witness to Henry's open affair with next wife-to-be Anne Boleyn (and before that, with a few other women).

At long last, on May 23, 1533, the final deed was done: Catharine found herself short one husband and one marriage after a special court—one more than just slightly stacked against her—granted Henry his long-sought annulment.[7]

Whether it was failed Plan A or the new Plan B, however, it was clear that Henry felt compelled to submit to the long, arduous task of building an explicit written legal and political case for getting out from under his marriage commitment to Catharine (and his later wives), rather than merely walking away from his vow, oath or promise to love, honor and cherish, or (hint!) his commitment actually to do all that stuff.

In fact, every last campaign to rid himself of his current wife, except the last (when Catharine Parr outlived him), took months, sometimes years, and were the exact opposite of someone simply pulling out a sabre, cutting someone's head off, and dumping the body in the woods.

Historians have amply detailed all the hoops that Henry had to jump through for moving on to each of his next five wives. Why all that royal effort? Henry and his court knew commitments when they saw them, and understood full well that they were far more than mere vows or promises—and indeed far more complex. As a consequence, while King and Court weren't trying hard to define commitments, they felt immense pressure, and thus worked day and night sometimes for years, to find the right language and the right approvals to get out from under them.

They did all this in the profound belief that, even though folks still hadn't gotten around to defining the word very well, commitments were real, and that they couldn't make them disappear simply with one fell stroke of a pen—or a sword.

Why did they believe that?

5. Can the Silver Screen Tell Us What Commitments Are?

If she wanted out of the marriage commitment, so be it, I made clear in my self-authored legal briefs. It should be a fifty-fifty split, and neatly written down for the judge were all the reasons why.

B's lawyers salivated at first. This guy, they said, was going to defend himself before a woman judge and his "wronged" wife *and* her two women lawyers?

Oh how they all were going to eat me up and spit me out!

******

Two burly cops were standing on the stoop when I opened the door of my Georgetown home. They had a court order in hand, so they said. Somberly, the one closest to me said I had to leave my house immediately. The other, holding a piece of paper tautly much like town criers of long ago, was so far back that I could not see what was written on it at all. No question that I was dumb to what was going on, but not quite that dumb. If I wanted to read the court order, they insisted, I would have to step out of the house. I told them they were welcome to come in, but I wasn't stepping out anywhere.

A blur then, more of a dirtier blur now, the door where the cops stood on the stoop, such a seemingly innocuous place for me to learn a hard lesson about what commitments were…and weren't.

In the end, I did pack a bag and leave when, in hindsight, I probably should have just slammed the door in their faces. As any divorce lawyer and the many men and women targeted by an unhappy spouse can confirm, a classic shadow play was unfolding. Unbeknownst to me, my then-wife B had started a covert process, urged on by our neighbor, a top Washington, D.C. divorce attorney, to dump me and lay claim to most of the money and assets we jointly owned.

Or so she and her attorney thought. Unlike so many of these sad and sorry tales, my story does not end with me crying about injustice.

Far from it. Thanks to my laptop and the Internet, it wasn't too long before I became wise to the scripts that my wife's high-end divorce lawyer had so expertly begun to follow. With that knowledge, I beat B and her coterie of law-school geniuses at their own game.

If she wanted out of the marriage commitment, so be it, I made clear in my self-authored legal briefs. It should be a fifty-fifty split, and neatly written down for the judge were all the reasons why.

B's lawyers salivated at first. This guy, they said, was going to defend himself before a woman judge and his "wronged" wife *and* her two women lawyers?

Oh how they all were going to eat me up and spit me out!

Eight expensive-for-*her* months later, B and her lawyers were not laughing any more. Little did any of us know that the judge would look upon B's lawyer's playbook with as little relish as I did. Nor did they know the judge had about as much patience with B's legal team as a New York City taxicab driver does with out-of-town tourists driving slowly in front of the cab just to take in the sights.

In her great wisdom, the judge ordered exactly the 50-50 split I had defined, accepting my proposal with nary a word changed. I paid no legal fees, while B came away from her juridical campaign about $40,000 worse for wear. Her lawyer sure won: I hear that she took two vacations to the Caribbean and one more to Europe, all on B's dime. Ironically, B and I could have come up with the same fifty-fifty solution for about $300 in court costs if she had simply said: "I want out!"

Ah, greed! Ah, simplicity! Isn't it amazing how often you end up screwing yourself when you work so hard to screw someone else? Just how much overkill do you really need to kill a commitment?

Any intelligent fool can make things bigger, more complex, and more violent. It takes a touch of genius— and a lot of courage—to move in the opposite direction.

E.F. Schumacher

Breaking up is just hard, even if you're the one breaking up. It's not fun. It can be dramatic and complicated. And then you get a little distance and you think, why did it have to be so complicated and dramatic?

Norah Jones

Making the simple complicated is commonplace; making the complicated simple, awesomely simple, that's creativity.

Charles Mingus

We all have big changes in our lives that are more or less a second chance.

Harrison Ford

Some commitments are so strong...

...that neither swords nor armies are strong enough to break them—yet mere words on a piece of paper can rip them apart! If, though, commitments are at once both incredibly strong and so profoundly vulnerable to spoken or written words, how is it that we have come to rely so heavily on them?

Maybe movies can tell us. To find out, let's adjust the dials on the wayback machine once again, this time to move forward to New York City in 1940 and then to Washington, D.C. in 1988. Maybe there we can find out a bit more, not only about what commitments are but also *why* we rely on them so much.

Our first stop is New York City's magnificent Radio City Music Hall and the world premiere of a new MGM comedy, *The Philadelphia Story*, on December 26, 1940. The very next day, the *New York Times* raved:

> "All those folks who wrote Santa Claus asking him to send them a sleek new custom-built comedy with fast lines and the very finest in Hollywood fittings got their wish just one day late with the opening of 'The Philadelphia Story' yesterday at the Music Hall.

> "For, this [Christmas] present, which really comes via Metro-Goldwyn-Mayer, has just about everything that a blue-chip comedy should have—a witty, romantic script derived by Donald Ogden Stewart out of Philip Barry's successful play; the flavor of high-society elegance, in which the patrons invariably luxuriate, and a splendid cast of performers headed by Katharine Hepburn, James Stewart and Cary Grant.

"Money and talent are mostly going these days into elaborate outdoor epics and rugged individualist films. It is like old times to see one about the trials and tribulations of the rich, and to have Miss Hepburn back, after a two-year recess, as [the] spoiled and willful daughter of America's unofficial peerage, comporting herself easily amid swimming pools, stables and the usual appurtenances of a huge estate."

What were those "trials and tribulations of the rich" to which the much respected *New York Times* film critic Bosley Crowther was referring?

Well, the story line of *The Philadelphia Story* was indeed clever. Young, wealthy, beautiful, recently-divorced, and amazingly snobby Philadelphia socialite Tracy Lord, superbly portrayed by Katharine Hepburn, was about to marry a boring but equally snobby fellow, George Kittredge (played by the then-well known actor John Howard).

Alas, poor George backed out on the wedding day, stiff upper lip and all. He simply could not tolerate his bride-to-be's "scandalous" if totally innocent midnight swim the night before with rag sheet reporter Macaulay "Mike" Connor (Jimmy Stewart).

How did that come about? Reporter Mike had been at Tracy Lord's castle-like Philadelphia mansion for days, along with his cynical almost-girlfriend, paparazzi sidekick Liz Imbrie (brought to life by the remarkable Ruth Hussey). Nominally, Mike and Liz were there to cover the upcoming wedding of socialite Tracy. But they had actually shoehorned their way into the Lord homestead on a mission to smoke out the real truth—and likely scandal—behind rumors that Tracy Lord's sixty-year-old-or-so father Seth (John Halliday) was living it up and, horror of horrors back in the late 1930s, actually living *with* a beautiful young Russian dancer 90 miles north in New York City.

How did socialite Tracy and reporter Mike end up in that swimming pool on the eve of the wedding? A few drinks had helped them along the way, as had vulnerable Mike's infatuation with Tracy. Worse still, and adding to everyone's chagrin, Tracy's ex-husband, C. K. Dexter Haven, admirably played by a dashing young Cary Grant, had also crashed the wedding preparations in hopes of reclaiming the bride-to-be as his own again, making everything even more confused for Tracy—and certainly more frustrating for straight-laced groom-to-be George.

On the morning after Tracy and Mike's midnight romp, push came to shove quite literally at the breakfast table just before the wedding ceremony: the instant George found out about the midnight swim, he punched poor Mike right in the nose and stalked off in a huff, leaving behind the marriage ceremony—and Tracy. What an opening for ex-hubby Dexter to win over Tracy's heart a second time! Which is exactly what he did in record time, taking George's place at the altar just minutes later to marry a very willing Tracy for the second time around! Audiences always shed a tear at that moment. If they're not cheering, that is.

Alas, Dexter's coming to Tracy's rescue was initially to Reporter Mike's mortifying chagrin, given his crush on the young Philadelphia beauty. Ah, but you know how Hollywood works: it took Mike only minutes to recover and find happiness with (you guessed it!) co-worker Liz. Audiences usually shed a tear at that moment, too.

My synopsis does no justice to the extraordinary acting, cinematography and creativity overflowing in *The Philadelphia Story*. Having garnered six Academy Award nominations and two wins, one for Stewart and the other for screenwriter Donald Ogden Stewart, *The Philadelphia Story* is a true film classic, a must-see. If you haven't yet discovered this milestone in American cinema, put this book down now, find the movie at the library or on the Web, watch it, and then come on back.[8]

"Ah," you may ask, "but what does *The Philadelphia Story* tell us about commitment?

On the surface, one answer might easily suggest itself: both father Seth and daughter Tracy had broken commitments to their spouses, one by "living in sin," as they used to put it back then, and the other by divorce. Yet this is not the critical element of commitment uncovered by *The Philadelphia Story*.

Instead, it is the film's stark if subtle confirmation that American society—long before 1940—knew a commitment when it saw one even though there was no agreed definition then as now. Moreover, Americans had long become conditioned to accept—as quite normal—broken marriage commitments without batting an eyelash, and also knew how costly and complicated it could be to break them.

In a word, while there is great creativity, acting and cinematic art in *The Philadelphia Story*, there was no new "news" in its message either that there were such things as commitments, or that commitments were made to be broken. All this said, no one still quite knew what those commitments were *really* made of.

Another more vexing issue arises regarding what commitments were—or are: if Tracy actually divorced Dexter even before we are introduced to these two young Philadelphia patricians, why did she marry him again? After all, why we make commitments, break them, and then make them all over again is what this book is supposed to explain.

To find at least part of the answer, let's make our way forward in time to 1988 and *The War of the Roses*. I'm referring not to English history and instead to the black comedy starring Michael Douglas, Danny DeVito and Kathleen Turner, directed by none other than DeVito himself. This jarring two-hour exploration of commitments made and broken depicts the catastrophic blood-curdling breakup of a marriage between two wealthy, tenacious, smart, self-entitled people, Oliver and Barbara Rose (Douglas and Turner, respectively).

We learn of this tragedy through the story-telling of divorce attorney Gavin d'Amato (DeVito), who at film's opening is recounting the epic battle between the Roses to a new client ruefully contemplating divorce. As lawyer d'Amato depicts them, Oliver and Barbara Rose would do anything to come out on top in their internecine battle over who was to get what possessions from their failed marriage. The movie's stark ending is a reminder that even commitments as strongly held as the Roses' are oftentimes not easily broken even when everyone involved demands that they must come to an end.

Obvious but never explicitly stated in *War of the Roses* is the undercurrent theme from the book of the same name, authored by Warren Adler and published in 1981. No slouch when it comes to acid social commentary, Adler has written 33 books over the past 50 years depicting human nature and the passionate drive of people in conflict.

To quote from the author's own online bio: "Adler's themes deal primarily with intimate human relationships, the mysterious nature of love and attraction, the fragile relationships between husbands and wives and parents and children, the corrupting power of money, the aging process, and how families cling together when challenged by the outside world."

Adler's savage *War of the Roses* saga, of a well-off couple descending into a maelstrom of self-destruction, does more than that, however, by providing insight into what commitments are and why we make them. Unfortunately, I can go only so far to explain exactly how and why without disclosing the jaw-dropping end to the story, both as Adler wrote it and as the actors extravagantly portrayed it.

This much can be said: each protagonist, Oliver and Barbara, was hell-bent on clinging to the other as the only remaining option for getting what the other had committed to give...but hadn't. Rather than pushing away one another, they were determined not to let go of each another until each actually delivered the promised goods—or else!

And what an "or else" it was! In that astonishing moment towards film's end lies the critical clue that *War of the Roses* offers about why we make commitments: commitments center on actually delivering the goods, not just promising to do so, and our *wanting* those goods is the core reason why we make commitments in the first place.

Readers and reviewers of Adler's novel and the film usually don't pick up on this. They have traditionally described *War of the Roses* as a tragic tale of two people corrupted by wealth, money and power who, finding themselves besotted by the emptiness of a once passionate relationship, decide that the second best thing they can achieve is to walk away from the marriage with as many material goods and as much cash as possible, each at the other's expense.

Or, critics will assert, Adler was writing about the predictable and costly moral destruction of people brought on by their wealth, and the horrid impact of divorce on the lives of children. Others will claim that Adler was portraying people whose personalities and self-identity were so weak that they could define themselves only by the expensive and extravagant cars they owned or how much money was in their bank accounts.

Still others argue that the "real" truth in Adler's caustic morality play is that each Rose promised the other a rose garden (did I really say that?), didn't deliver the expected floral landscape, and became convinced that the other spouse "had totally wasted my life" during 20 years of marriage. As a result, each spouse was going to pay a heavy penalty indeed for non-delivery.

Remember what we Brooklynites say? "Yer pays yer money and makes yer choice!" It can be any of those things, or any combination of them. However, missing in these explanations is this: just as did *The Philadelphia Story* and the saga of Henry VIII, Adler's *War of the Roses* recounts a sad tale of unmet expectations after two people made a commitment that had them believing they would get far more out of the deal than they actually got.

As ordinary as sliced white bread as this chain of events is, let's focus on discovering its true meaning. With the passing of days, weeks, months or years after it is made, our understanding inevitably changes as to what the commitment was originally meant to do, just like the way our hearing or vision or memory blurs as time passes.

The unique circumstances of the Roses, Tracy Lord, and even Henry VIII drive home a point otherwise easily overlooked: any commitment that you make or receive inevitably will be broken unless you are willing to modify it the same way you adjust to your body's changes over time. Tuck this "need for change" away in your mind along with "future" and "emotionally impelled." Like those two earlier concepts, we'll come back to the consequences of "change" soon enough.

For now, let's return just for a moment to *The Philadelphia Story*.

When they first married, young Tracy Lord (Katharine Hepburn) and C. K. Dexter Haven (Cary Grant) not only thought that they were making their first-round love-honor-and-cherish commitments with eyes wide open, but also that their expectations for the other *to deliver on those commitments* were wholly reasonable.

Unhappily, they eventually uncovered the bad news: that those commitments from their first wedding were not going to be honored and "delivery" was not going to be made. Why? Because they found out that their expectations of one another for sustained delivery in fact were *not* reasonable. How? Learning by doing...actually learning by *not* doing. Neither one was capable of delivering *to* the other what each of the two had originally committed to deliver. Dexter drank too much, and Tracy...well, take my word for it right now and see the film to find out why for yourself.

Which brings us to the heart of the matter: whenever a delivery borne of a commitment no longer seems possible for whatever reason, the first option is to modify the commitment if you really want to continue living or working with the person who originally agreed to deliver the goods. Maybe that will be easy, or maybe it will be hard. Either way, it is the soundest of first steps to take.

You see soon enough in *The Philadelphia Story* why this first option, modifying the commitment, didn't fit well with Tracy and Dexter's first marriage. So they each wisely deferred to the second option: each one lets go of his or her hold on the other to "deliver the goods" and then simply moves on, lessons hopefully learned. Also easy to say and hard to do.

Tracy and Dexter opted for ending their first marriage because they accepted two stark truths. The first? That the hoped-for outcome to their first marriage commitment had proven itself out of reach. The second? Individually on their own, each had decided, wisely or not, that it was no longer in his or her personal self-interest to work together to make the promised delivery to one another. So, they concluded, the time had come to file for an orderly "commitment bankruptcy" in which each would let the other off the hook rather than engaging in a combat mission destined to fail.

Notably as they embarked on their second marriage, Tracy and Dexter were far more sensitive to an unmistakable requirement which became self-evident only as a result of their failed first marriage: to be much more realistic the second time around about their capacity to deliver the goods that went missing in their first marriage. In effect, they were underscoring the reality that in their new commitment, as in any commitment, the participants must do more than just promise something; they must be as realistic as possible—before they make the commitment—when judging their ability to come up with and deliver results, all without over-promising. Hardly easy to do, it is always worth the effort, even if the results will never be perfect.

Oliver and Barbara Rose couldn't abide the first option—modifying their original commitment—or the second option—ending it altogether. In the most darkly comic way, they played a devil's game by choosing a third option: abandoning their original marriage commitment *to* each other but demanding *from* each other every last delivery of every last thing that each one had originally committed to deliver to the other. You give, I take. What's mine is mine and what's yours is mine, too!

In taking this fool's game course, they overlooked both of two elements common to all commitments: first, the mother of all "whys" of commitments, namely that we make commitments with other people to get what we want *from* those people (a feature taken up later in this book in detail), and second, that everyone agreeing to the commitment has to work together in common purpose, not against one another, if any one of them is to be able to deliver what any of the others want.

Enough said? Not quite. Each of these stories—Henry VIII, *The Philadelphia Story,* and *The War of the Roses*—actually points to yet another *why* among the whys of making commitments.

This particular "why" centers on the importance of "delivering the goods." We make commitments not only because we want something from someone else but because delivering something to someone else is the only way we can get back what we want.

Want more proof? Let's stop thinking marriages and instead start thinking music, like maybe *The Beatles!*

COMMITMENTS

6. Commitments and What The Beatles Tell Us

Days passed. Then weeks. Then months. How we hung on, I don't know. Without a cent to the company's name and with rent and other bills past due, the day finally came when my wife and I sat down to discuss when to pull the plug on our business. Two weeks had already gone by since the last of too many calls to and from Citibank Germany. "Yes," they assured us. "We're going to do business with you. The check will be in the mail soon."

Still no check.

******

In 1979, after leaving the State Department, I started a consulting business. It caught on, and by the mid-1980s, every major bank in the United States was using one or another of our services to keep on top of Washington: newsletters, reports, white papers, and even the rudimentary beginnings of electronic messaging via a now-ancient computer-to-computer system called RBBS.

How quickly things can change. As it turns out, we were a luxury for our clients, not a necessity. During the financial crisis of the mid- and late-1980s, as banks and savings-and-loans tumbled one after another, our client list and revenues shrank faster than a thoroughbred out of the gate. So, too, did our enthusiasm for keeping a business alive that was seemingly destined to fail.

Then, in 1989, as the Soviet Union and its puppet allies in Eastern Europe began to disintegrate as a united political force, I made a last-ditch attempt to parlay my long-unused professional network in the Soviet Bloc empire into a valuable commodity. In the belief that I could help Citibank open banks there, and without even knowing whether it wanted to, I penned a two sentence letter to then-Citibank CEO John Reed about how it *should* want them there, and that we could help them pull it off as no one else could.

As it turned out, that was exactly what Reed did want to do! He sent a handwritten endorsement of us to the Citibank officer in charge of Europe, and it wasn't long before I was negotiating with Citibank officers in charge of Belgium, Italy, and Germany, to guide them in opening banks in Poland, Hungary and Czechoslovakia. Settling on a fair price, it sure looked to us in Washington as if our phoenix was rising from the ashes. Citibank's business had come in the nick of time, too, since we were just about out of money.

Days passed. Then weeks. Then months. How we hung on, I don't know. Without a cent to the company's name and with rent and other bills past due, the day finally came when my wife and I sat down to discuss when to pull the plug on our business. Two weeks had already gone by since the last of too many calls to and from Citibank Germany. "Yes," they assured us. "We're going to do business with you. The check will be in the mail soon."

Still no check.

I can't remember exactly how the conversation went, but the decision my wife and I reached that morning is chiseled in my memory: We'll wait one more day, for tomorrow's mail, and if the check's not there, we'll hang it all up.

Citibank's check for $50,000 was in the next day's mail. It presaged a year of challenges galore as our team worked with Citibank in Europe to secure agreement from the Czechoslovak government and Czechoslovak Central Bank for Citibank to open for business in Prague.

Citibank branch and ATM in Prague. So simple, so ordinary. Yet, less than two decades ago, it didn't exist. Or anything like it. I wouldn't have traded any other business opportunity for the one to chase down and land the Czechoslovak government "OK" to open these doors.

There were two miracles: the first, of course, our receiving the $50,000 check on the very day we needed it the most. The second? A critical "Yes" on the dotted line, a year later, at the very end of a forty-five minute one-on-one negotiation with a tough-as-nails Czechoslovak Finance Minister (later, its President) Vaclav Klaus, who came into the room with a "No!" written all over his face.

Wait a minute. *Wait a minute!* The check as a miracle? I need to take that back.

For that envelope to have arrived that day, people somewhere, and certainly weeks beforehand, had to have put signatures to contracts, signed a disbursement order, printed a check, and put it in the German mail. Those are not the elements of a miracle, but rather the makings of a predictably slow bureaucratic process. Maybe one that made us sweat a lot, but predictable nonetheless.

What has stayed with me to this day is the real miracle: that the two of us were smart enough to sit down and act on our longstanding commitment to face the grim reality if it ever looked like the company would have to be shut down. That afternoon, we soberly talked through what we would do if we folded that day, the next, or somehow went on for more than that, and even how we would face telling Citibank that we were no longer able to deliver the goods we had promised.

In the end, we won because we followed that commitment playbook to the letter.

The measure of intelligence is the ability to change.
Albert Einstein

The human capacity for burden is like bamboo—far more flexible than you'd ever believe at first glance.
Jodi Picoult, My Sister's Keeper

The boldness of asking deep questions may require unforeseen flexibility if we are to accept the answers.
Brian Greene

The good news is, we're not bankrupt. The bad news is, we're close.
Richard J. Codey

So, we're saying...

...that a common element in any commitment is "delivering the goods."

Oh those Beatles! Did they ever deliver!

Or did they?

That legendary British "boy band" of the 1960s gave us a style and sound of music that endures, appealing not only to Baby Boomers like me but also to the younger GenXers who followed my generation, and even today's Millennials who are usually transfixed (for good reason!) by artists of the likes of Justin Timberlake, Lady Gaga, Usher, Beyonce, Blake Shelton, Alicia Keys, Taylor Swift, Adele, Carrie Underwood, Zac Brown Band, Kenny Chesney, Maroon Five, and Lady Antebellum.

Eventual world renown may not have been self-evident to the Beatles' George Harrison, Paul McCartney, Ringo Starr (eventually), and John Lennon when the group started out in the 1950s as the Quarrymen covering the likes of Buddy Holly's *That'll Be The Day*. By the early 1960s, however, success and notoriety first in England and then in Germany was coming fast. And then, following their triumphant early-1964 conquest of the United States, the four musicians were openly professing a lifetime commitment to their incarnation as The Beatles.

Alas, by 1970, only six years later, The Beatles' commitment to one another had crumbled, in the wake of each Beatle having charted his own individual musical career, his own distinct persona, and his own albums and singles. The final blow came on December 31 of that year, when Paul McCartney filed suit in Britain against his former Beatles colleagues, their manager, and one of the agents responsible for the group's commercial success.

Was the Beatles' demise inevitable? Having so successfully fostered a lasting musical legacy, one as compelling today as when they first came on the scene, were the Beatles fated to break their commitments to each other and to their common success?

There is little doubt that, when the "Fab Four" (as they came to be known) first put their names on agreements in the mid-1960s to collaborate, they meant to commit to one another in complete harmony. Unfortunately, during the years to follow, the four drifted apart spiritually and physically, torn by internal rivalries or the alleged bad influence of this Beatle's wife or that Beatle's girlfriend.

What did Starr, Lennon, McCartney and Harrison really let go of when The Beatles fell apart? One answer is clear enough: they let go of their commitments to one another. When the last straw actually broke the camel's back may never be known: in his 1970 law suit, McCartney explicitly claimed that everyone in the group already had known for a long time that The Beatles had been ripped off and torn apart by mismanagement, misappropriation of funds, and unpaid royalties.

Above all, The Beatles were unhappily letting go of something far more crippling than these alleged misdeeds: they were abandoning the self-imposed rigidity imposed by an initial commitment to channel, package and present all of their creativity in just one single formulaic identity—The Beatles—that was destined to constrain their growth, maturity and financial reward as distinctly unique individuals.

The Beatles hardly invented this way of falling apart. In the music industry alone, over the three prior decades preceding the Beatles' emergence, the same story already had unfolded again and again: the Dorsey Brothers' breakup, Billie Holiday's loss of royalties, and the 1942 strike over royalty payments by just about every big name in the business, including Count Basie, Woody Herman, Judy Garland, Bing Crosby, Benny Goodman, Kay Kyser, Dinah Shore, Spike Jones and Duke Ellington. Hundreds of commitments anchored in formulaic "group" solutions. Hundreds of commitments broken.

In a powerful homage late in 1979, Time Magazine was to declare that "no other group has ever pushed rock so far, or asked so much from it." The newsweekly was not speaking of The Beatles and instead referring to *The Who*. Time Magazine was not alone: according to *Rolling Stone:* "Along with The Beatles and The Rolling Stones, The Who complete the holy trinity of British rock."

High praise indeed. And well deserved, too! Unlike The Beatles, part of our admiration for The Who lies in universal recognition that unlike the Beatles, The Who's Roger Daltrey (lead vocals, guitar, harmonica), Pete Townshend (guitar, vocals, keyboards), John Entwistle (bass, vocals) and Keith Moon (drums, vocals) managed to build something destined to last more than 50 years, even though the participants went their own creative ways or even passed away during those same decades.

The foundation for The Who's remarkable commitment to one another was everyone's willingness to adjust rather than abandon their joint commitment to the brand and creativity that was uniquely The Who. Their flexibility in keeping that commitment alive was a key ingredient in the formula for making The Who's brand grow, prosper and stick despite changing times and expectations.

You will find out lots more about the importance of flexibility in commitments later on. It suffices for now simply to say that The Who pulled off this success despite no end of pulling and tugging from within and without: Moon's early passing at age 32 in 1978, disbanding the group in 1983 without rancor or lawsuits, reuniting as The Who for the 1985 Live Aid Concert, worldwide reunion tours over the 20 years to follow, induction into the Rock and Roll Hall of Fame in 1990, releases like the top-ten 2006 album *Endless Wire,* and fabulous concert appearances right up through 2012 at the London Olympics and the Concert for Sandy Relief.

That The Who are still able to come together over the decades—in effect, serially recommitting to one another—is testimony to how commitments can and do survive by evolving, just like the people who make them. And to how it can be done without rancor. Indeed, the band has added new members, such as drummer Kenney Jones, to keep the brand alive and the rhythm flowing. Go you guys!

The story is much the same with the Rolling Stones.

Still performing together after a half century to the sheer delight of worldwide audiences young and old—witness the Stones' June, 2013 Fiftieth Anniversary Concert in Glastonbury, England—Mick Jagger and company appear to be taking as much pleasure now as they did in 1963 when they began creating the Rolling Stones' unique vocal and instrumental harmonies. Whatever it has taken to keep their commitment alive, it truly has been well worth the effort for them, and a lasting source of pleasure for the rest of us.

The Bee Gees, too, enjoyed a nearly 40 year run, giving credence to the notion that family ties may help music group members keep their commitments to one another.

Then again, they may not. Tommy and Jimmy Dorsey split up their single orchestra in 1935 and rancorously competed head-to-head with separate bands for the next ten years. And how about the lasting tensions within the late Michael Jackson's family? Or the Jonas' Brothers?

By these measures, blood ties are not at all the secret sauce for keeping commitments alive. So it must be something else.

COMMITMENTS

7. Commitments, Laundry Detergent, Ice Cream and the Great White Way

More nanoseconds. I fly and then thrust an arm into the narrowing space to stop the doors from slamming shut. Thank God they part magically, and my arm is still attached to the rest of me.

And then there he is, his back up against the far wall of the elevator cab, empty except for him, with me standing between the doors now slamming against me, trying to close. Beep! Bump. Beep! Bump. Stupidly funny all this, had I not been so, so angry...

"Whatareyah doin', man?" he slurs. "What's it to you?"

******

The sounds are unmistakable: rubber screeching on hot black asphalt, the crash of metal against metal, the screams. Oh, God, the screams!

Heads turn. A bloodied woman tumbles to the pavement from the driver's seat, her door wrenched open from the impact of a rear-end collision. The little red car behind hers had not stopped in time. The screaming continues, but the woman is silent in her agony, so where is that horrible wailing coming from? And then we see: in this time before seat belts and baby seats, her infant child has been thrown sideways, lying where its mother once sat, bleeding and shrieking.

The intersection of 14th and K in springtime downtown Washington D.C. is too busy at noontime for there to be any shortage of instant heroes swarming to the wreckage. The mother is now cradled in someone's arms, her red-soaked infant child gently picked up off the seat by a passerby turned gracious savior.

Where is the driver of that second car, the one that rear-ended the first?

Then I see: where bent metal merges with broken glass on the driver's door, there suddenly appears a head, then arms, a thin young fellow. My God, was he dying, too?

14th & K. People in their own world, and I'm fighting my way through their indifference, chasing a lowlife who left two bloodied people on the pavement...

Nanoseconds. It is all happening in nanoseconds. His door opens. What vision of ripped flesh am I about to see? And why is no one else even looking at him? Enough people are helping mother and child; I'll help him!

Before I even begin to move, he comes out. No blood, thank God! Wait a minute! Where's he going? He's walking away, away from the gore, slowly, now faster, now fast. Why, that son of a bitch is making a break for it. And no one is watching. No one is seeing this happen!

He crosses over to my side of the street, oblivious to me. He makes it across the park, then an intersection, at a quickened pace. Over my dead body, I say to myself, so I follow him. He turns a corner, perhaps believing that he's pulled it off. The guy still doesn't see me. Then, halfway down the block, he suddenly does.

Now the creep is running, and I'm running after him. There are too many bodies in this noontime crowd, too many people going in and out of office buildings. Get out of the way! I can't let him lose me!

He turns left at the corner. I'm maybe two seconds behind, but he's disappeared. Damn it! There's a building entrance to my left. That has to be where he went. I dash inside. But I don't see him. I don't see elevators, either. No stairs. No escalators. And no runaway creep. More nanoseconds fly by. WHERE IS HE?

Then I get it: people are walking into the main lobby from around an inner corner. Maybe the stairs are there. I dash that way. There are no stairs, but there are four elevators, and the doors on the last on the left are just starting to close.

More nanoseconds. I fly and then thrust an arm into the narrowing space to stop the doors from slamming shut. Thank God they part magically, and my arm is still attached to the rest of me.

And then there he is, his back up against the far wall of the elevator cab, empty except for him, with me standing between the doors now slamming against me, trying to close. Beep! Bump. Beep! Bump. Stupidly funny all this, had I not been so, so angry…

"Whatareyah doin', man?" he slurs. "What's it to you?"

What now? He's stone-cold drunk, maybe stoned, and suddenly I don't have any idea what to do next. What if he has a gun? Or a knife? We're both out of sight of anyone in the main lobby, which now seems miles away.

"Police! Help! Call the police! I need help here!" I'm screaming. A few more nanoseconds pass. Then a security guard as big as a tackle for the New York Giants comes running around the corner. And I am loving it, loving him, and loving the whole world: there *is* a God!

After the cops take the guy away in handcuffs, a sergeant comes over to thank me for my civic duty. He tells me that the woman and child will be OK. But the officer's real purpose, he says, is to ask me just two questions: Why did I chase the creep down? (I could've been killed, he reminds me.) And, who was the woman to me?

Who *was* the woman to me? Or her infant child? Even though we had never met and to this day I still don't know their names, how did I know my commitment to them existed? How did I know that it was real and unshakeable? How did I know that I had to act, no matter what risk I was running?

Action is eloquence.

William Shakespeare

Talk doesn't cook rice.

Chinese Proverb

Action is the antidote to despair.

Joan Baez

Remember, people will judge you by your actions, not your intentions. You may have a heart of gold—but so does a hard-boiled egg.

Author Unknown

If rock bands are any indication...

...as many commitments fail as succeed. As we learned with The Who and the Rolling Stones, flexibility may be a key element in the formula for a commitment's success.

Maybe.

Time for more name dropping, so I'll drop these: William Procter, James Gamble, Iams pet foods, Duracell batteries, Braun shavers, Christina Aguilera Perfumes, and Tide laundry detergent—which I have purposefully crowded together in this half sentence. Evan Williams, Biz Stone and Twitter. Ben Cohen, Jerry Greenfield and ice cream. Gordon Moore, Bob Noyce and computer chips. Richard Rodgers, Oscar Hammerstein, *Oklahoma!*, *Carousel*, *South Pacific*, *The King and I*, *Flower Drum Song*, *The Sound of Music*, and more.

All these people. All these things. Each unique in touch, sight, sound and taste. Yet despite their inherent differences, all represent one thing in common: commitments that worked.

Some of these commitments have already lasted well beyond the lifetime of the people originally making them. Others were originally intended to last just a few months or years, like the Broadway productions created by Rodgers and Hammerstein. The jury's still out on whether one of these, Twitter, will last a lifetime, though right now everything points to a resounding "Yes!"

At the core of what I am talking about here is that people make commitments to one another to achieve a specific goal during a specific time period by doing certain things...by taking action.

Goals. Time. Action.

The *goal* can be finite, meaning we will build and sell this computer chip or sell that ice cream. Or, it can be centered on something truly intangible, as in building a brand like Proctor & Gamble even though you'll never see on store shelves any Proctor & Gamble batteries (they're Duracell!), Proctor & Gamble pet food (that's Iams!), Proctor & Gamble perfume (Christina Aguilera Perfumes and others besides), Proctor & Gamble shavers (think Braun) or Proctor & Gamble soap (Tide and many, many more laundry and cleaning brands everyone knows!).

As for *time*, it can be as short as it takes to fix a refrigerator, change the oil in the car, compose a Broadway musical and bring it to the stage, or as long as forever, like loving, honoring, and cherishing till death do us part.

The third element, *action*, is too often overlooked or unrecognized: doing all that is needed to get from here to there, that is, to the goal.

In an excellent summary of notable corporate partnerships,[9] Alyson Shontell hits the nail on the head writing of people who successfully committed to their companies' success:

> "Not surprisingly, many were long-time friends, classmates, or relatives. Others, however, did not get along initially. Some still are not amicable, despite their joint achievements. [Yet] there is a common trend: *the most well-rounded pairs recognized their individual limitations and respected what the other could bring to a partnership.*" [italics mine]

Shontell goes on to define what in her opinion (and mine) made the core partnerships work in Twitter, Ben & Jerry's, Intel, and Proctor & Gamble. We start with Twitter:

> "Evan Williams and Biz Stone joined forces to found Twitter after working at Blogger when it was sold to Google. Under Google's new reign, Williams hired Stone. "We started out as rivals but became great friends. We really respected each other. When

> Evan left [Google for Odeo.com] I was like, 'What??
> You're leaving me?' So I followed him." The pair was
> then approached by Jack Dorsey, an Odeo engineer
> with an idea. This discussion developed into Twitter,
> and the rest is history."

According to Shontell, their partnership works because Stone and Williams respect and trust each other.

> "Having both spent a decade in the blogging
> business, Stone and Williams are equally
> knowledgeable about the platform. Williams realized
> Twitter's potential and entrusted Stone with the
> micro-blogging site as a side project. Mutual respect,
> camaraderie and ambition have encouraged the two
> to stick together and achieve business success."

Well said.

Ben Cohen and Jerry Greenfield are the creators of my favorite ice cream, New York Super Fudge Chunk. (Don't tell my doctor!)

Cohen and Greenfield committed in 1978 to form an enterprise that for decades since has been bringing yummy to everyone's tummy. Friends since childhood, the two had enrolled in an ice-cream making correspondence course in 1977 and, after mastering it, made a $12,000 leap of faith investment to open their first ice cream shop, Ben & Jerry's.

The real faith in that leap was not the $12,000. Instead, it was anchored in themselves, in their friendship which even to this day counts dearly for them both, in their capacity to recognize the value in their differing strengths and weaknesses, and finally in their determination to act, not just preach, about giving back to the community. They have mightily succeeded in keeping alive that commitment to their common success much to their own and their customers' delight.

Then there is Gordon Moore and Bob Noyce.

"Who?" you ask? Well, the next time you turn on your PC, smart phone, or goodness knows what else, take a moment to thank them both. Moore and Noyce were among the "Traitorous Eight"[10] semiconductor designers who in 1957 left Shockley Semiconductor Laboratory, a company unknown today because it went out of business shortly thereafter.

Moore and Noyce went on to form Intel, a company the whole world knows. They got there initially with the help of the other six Traitorous Eights, who jointly formed Fairchild Semiconductors in 1957 by putting their signatures on each of eight one-dollar bills—the entire written agreement among them all! Believe it or not, it then took Fairchild Semiconductors less than four years to become the market leader designing semiconductors.

By 1968, still with itchy feet, Moore and Noyce made a fateful decision to leverage their success at Fairchild by founding Intel which, in its first day of operations, brought the now legendary Andy Grove on board to run company operations. The rest of Intel's enviable progression to industry pre-eminence is history.

Both Moore and Noyce were technical whiz kids, two of eight young, otherwise laid-back engineers, restless and rebellious enough to go out on their collective own against the conventional wisdom of then-corporate America. Still, the two differed remarkably from one another.

Noyce, co-inventor of the microchip, was a true visionary who looked into the future and saw the potential for Intel to be the worldwide leader producing ever more powerful chips for all forms of computing.

Equally avid in technology but more the quiet-spoken geek, Moore had the special genius to conceive, design, build and tailor ever more powerful and smaller computer chips. Much like ice cream gurus Cohen and Greenfield, Moore gives true meaning to the notion of giving back to the community: he and his wife have given more than $800 million to Caltech and the University of California alone, and much more besides through the Gordon and Betty Moore Foundation.

Why did their commitment to Intel work? Noyce, co-inventor of the microchip, and Moore the technology genius, both saw great value in how they differed from one another, not how they resembled one another. They had the wisdom to make room for each to succeed at what he did best, all the more remarkable given the incredible pressure of daily challenges and setbacks inherent in building a business from scratch.

Where did they find the special wisdom to let each other do his respective thing? In their inner confidence that, whatever the other one was doing that day, he was doing it for the Intel whole, not just for his own self-interest. They not only trusted one another, but each day gave one another more reason to keep that trust alive.

On to laundry detergent.

Born in 1801 in England, London candle-maker and then Ohio bank clerk William Proctor came to America after his first entrepreneurial venture, a dry goods shop, was robbed the day after it opened in 1832, leaving him some $8,000 in debt—about $180,000 in today's money!

It was no secret back home in London that Proctor was leaving for America to escape that debt. He had departed England with his first wife who, alas, tragically died shortly after their arrival in Cincinnati. The young widower, completely on his own, soon turned to candle-making to supplement his meager clerk's salary.

Like Proctor, James Gamble was born in England in 1803, but to an Irish family. In 1819, his family with 16-year-old James in tow, emigrated to America. Alas, the teenage Gamble fell so violently ill while the group was crossing Ohio that the family had to end its journey in Cincinnati rather than continue on to Illinois. There in Cincinnati they stayed, with Gamble eventually apprenticing in a soap factory.

So it came to pass that, unbeknownst to each other, both Proctor and Gamble were in the same place at the same time. How did the two actually get together? Enter two sisters, love conquering all, and a lot of animal fat.

Already home to a large slaughterhouse industry, Cincinnati in the early 1800s was afloat in the fats and oils from rendering animal carcasses. These by-products were essential not only to making soap but to dipping candles. A prominent Cincinnati candle-maker of the day, Alexander Norris, was already purchasing large quantities for his own business. He also happened to have two lovely daughters, Olivia and Elizabeth Anne.

Lo and behold, Proctor and Olivia met, fell in love and married, as did Gamble and Elizabeth Anne. In 1837, when father-in-law Alexander saw that both Proctor and Gamble were competing heavily for the same raw ingredients, he proposed that they form a joint venture and even agreed to stake it.

Why did Proctor and Gamble's partnership work? Alyson Shontell neatly sums it up:

> "Family and business values brought them
> together. Procter and Gamble helped each other
> create mass quantities of their products which led to
> a distribution deal with the U.S. Army."

The rest, as they say, is history. In that single U.S. Army contract and so many more to follow, these two new business partners reaped the benefits of sticking to a commitment to their common success, especially after the Proctor children began leveraging their special talent at marketing and the Gamble family's prowess emerged at product selection and innovation. As different as these skills were, over the century to follow, they were constantly refined and improved by Procter, Gamble, their children and their grandchildren, to keep pace as peoples' tastes and market demand evolved, became more varied, but always remained centered on quality.

On to the Great White Way!

For 16 years in the 1940s and 1950s, Richard Rodgers and Oscar Hammerstein II collaborated time and again to produce the sheer Broadway magic that enchanted everyone then as it does now—and will do forever. Rodgers' music and Hammerstein's lyrics garnered 34 Tony Awards, 15 Academy Awards, two Pulitzer Prizes, and two

Grammys, beginning in 1943 with *Oklahoma!* and then continuing with *Carousel, South Pacific, The King and I, Flower Drum Song, The Sound of Music,* and more besides. Not bad for a duo who in fact had been competitors for New York audiences in the 1920s and 1930s in their separate partnerships with Lorenz Hart (Rodgers) and Jerome Kern (Hammerstein).

In fact, by the time the United States entered World War II in late 1941, Rodgers and Hart already had successfully collaborated for more than two decades on many Broadway hits including *A Connecticut Yankee* (1927), *Babes in Arms* (1937), *The Boys from Syracuse* (1938), and *Pal Joey* (1940), as well as many film projects.

Likewise, by the early 1940s, Hammerstein and Kern also had made a lasting name for themselves as a powerful creative partnership. Recognized early in the 1920s for *The Desert Song* (1926), Hammerstein began his successful collaboration with composer Kern on the hit *Sunny* (1925), afterwards following up with the less-well-received *Sweet Adeline* (1929) and *Very Warm for May* (1939).

Those last two were not hits. Little matter. By 1930, Hammerstein and Kern had been assigned by critics and the public to a league of their own for their ground-breaking smash hit *Show Boat,* which opened some 86 years ago in 1927 and is still considered one of the true masterpieces of American musical theatre.[11]

If Rodgers and Hart were a successful match, and Hammerstein and Kern were, too, how did Rodgers and Hammerstein come together? And why?

We can thank writer Lynn Riggs and her 1930 play *Green Grow the Lilacs.* A Pulitzer Prize-nominated production that had a critically successful if short Broadway run in early 1931, this all-but-forgotten word-and-folk-song exploration of frontier life in Oklahoma had appealed both to Rodgers and Hammerstein as a possible Broadway musical.

Oddly, this happened without each ever knowing at first that the other had been drawn to the concept. It was only after Hart, sinking ever more deeply into alcoholism, turned thumbs down on the idea with his partner Rodgers, and only after Kern had come to the same no-go decision with Hammerstein, that Rodgers and Hammerstein, then only acquaintances, sought out one another. The two immediately relished in their shared if independently conceived inspiration from *Green Grow the Lilacs.* Letting flow their combined if radically different creative skills, the two together penned *Oklahoma!,* and the show opened on Broadway on March 31, 1943 to near universal acclaim.[12]

How lucky we all are that they said yes to each other! *Oklahoma!* was followed by a string of more hits, including: *Carousel, South Pacific, The King and I, Flower Drum Song,* and *The Sound of Music,* their creative dynamic coming to an end only with Hammerstein's sudden passing in 1960 at age 65; Rodgers died years later at age 76 in 1979.

What was the nature of Rodgers and Hammerstein's commitment to one another? Well, it certainly wasn't close friendship, because in fact they never were close friends. Instead...well, we'll let their own words speak for themselves, on how they purposefully went out of their way to make room for one-another's unique creative genius:

> "He's a meticulously hard worker and yet he'll roam the grass of his farm for hours and sometimes for days before he can bring himself to put a word on paper." (Rodgers, the creative musical genius of the pair, referring to Hammerstein, the lyricist.)

> "I hand him a lyric and get out of his way." (Hammerstein, the creative lyrical genius of the pair, referring to Rodgers, the composer.)

Gordon Moore and Bob Noyce. Evan Williams and Biz Stone. Ben and Jerry. Rodgers and Hammerstein. These and myriad other stories of successful collaboration lead us to the inescapable conclusion that for commitments to work, their common ingredients must include a clear goal, enough time to achieve it, action, and enough room left by each for the other to do his or her own thing.

Goals. Time. Action. Room for each partner to do his or her own thing. Critical ingredients not only for making a commitment work, but also for having the confidence that a commitment even exists.

Sounds easy enough, right? Not so fast. As it turns out, we need more. Dare I say: "Trust me on this!"?

8. Commitments, Trust Well-Placed and Trust Misplaced!

I'm almost twelve years old. We're sitting in his brand new 1954 Chrysler. He's just picked me up from the Monday night Boy Scout meeting at Temple Israel. But instead of making the right turn onto Rockaway Turnpike to go the last block and a half to the house, he's stopped the car right at the bus stop on Central Avenue, not moving at all even though the light had turned green.

"Why have we stopped, Dad?"

******

I don't remember much from my childhood. These days, psychoanalysts might explain why by arguing that my family was so tortuously dysfunctional—by reason of bad genes or whatever—that I shouldn't be surprised at banishing my memories from consciousness. They might add: I ought not blame my parents too much and instead watch out for my own genetic code trip wires!

What a self-entitled twenty-first century notion that is! The truth is, my family life was full of daily venal anger, and it wasn't just genes, not by a long shot. Night after night, I had to retreat to the relative safety and darkness of a tiny bedroom, turning up the volume on my faithful little plug-in AM radio so that Jean Shepherd and his surreal fantasies could drown out the awful cursing and fighting between two very cocksure parents who had every right, they screamed, to take it out on one another every single day...and night.

Indeed, each evening like clockwork at around 10 pm, they descended into their self-created hellish whirlpool of mutual self-hatred. You'd think they'd get tired of the same script after a while. Alas, no. Those two parents of mine, creatures of habit as they were, had no imagination at all!

Yet if you were to ask me now, today, to share the actual dialogue of their vicious playbook script, I wouldn't be able to recall a single word. Yet I do remember this one subplot down to the very last syllable, much as if my father had been speaking to me only moments ago.

I'm almost twelve years old. We're sitting in his brand new 1954 Chrysler. He's just picked me up from the Monday night Boy Scout meeting at Temple Israel. But instead of making the right turn onto Rockaway Turnpike to go the last block and a half to the house, he's stopped the car right at the bus stop on Central Avenue, not moving at all even though the light had turned green.

"Why have we stopped, Dad?"

"There's something I need to tell you. I'm not coming home with you tonight. I'll be living in the city."

"You're not coming home?"

"No."

And with that, he slipped the car into drive, made the right turn, and drove the last few hundred yards in silence.

"You better get out." That is all he had to say once the car was in the driveway.

So I did.

For the next seven years, as my mother held on tightly and bitterly to a once-molding now rotted Swiss-cheese marriage and a long-gone husband, hostilities raged on between the two. My father was financially squeezing her and the rest of us dry in explicit retaliation for her refusing to agree to a divorce. Who would want to recall any of that, I ask myself even now. No wonder I don't remember much.

As easy as 1-2-3, they say. From Temple Israel (1), to the Central Avenue bus stop (2), to home (3). Such a short ride, such a short father-to-son message, but such long-lasting venom…the rabid hatred that my father destructively carried to his grave some 40 years later. For what purpose?

It was not until many years later that I realized how, in their tenacious warfare to keep each other in the greatest possible agony, they had violated a commitment to my sister, my brothers and me. They should have been looking out for us as their kids, even if they had the best of reasons not to want to look out for each other anymore.

As a child, how would I have known how natural it was to trust in my parents' commitment to us, or how strongly I had actually placed my faith directly in them? It took me a long time to piece together how much I had indeed counted on them, and just how badly I had misplaced that trust. Who knew?

How *do* we know when our trust is misplaced in someone who has made a commitment to us? All too often, we learn of our mistake only when it is too late to escape the damage done, much less in time to undo it.

And, alas, sometimes we never find out at all.

Trust your own instinct. Your mistakes might as well be your own, instead of someone else's.

Billy Wilder

Deciding whether or not to trust a person is like deciding whether or not to climb a tree, because you might get a wonderful view from the highest branch, or you might simply get covered in sap, and for this reason many people choose to spend their time alone and indoors, where it is harder to get a splinter.

Lemony Snicket

"A man who will steal for me will steal from me."
*Theodore Roosevelt, dismissing on the spot
one of his best cowhands who was about to claim
for his boss an unmarked animal.
Cited by David McCullough,
Mornings on Horseback*

As important as they are...

...a goal, time, and action aren't enough to make a commitment work.

So, what is missing?

Maybe we can look to politicians for the answer, those folks who promise us the sun, moon and sky. Or zero in on a small slice of legal history coupled with a subtle but real moment of racism that began unfolding on a railroad car in 1892, some 31 years after the end of slavery in the United States.

Let's do the latter first. We begin not in 1892, though, but 30 years earlier in 1863, during the American Civil War.

Just about everyone attending grade school in the United States learns that President Abraham Lincoln freed the slaves on January 1st of that year by signing the Emancipation Proclamation. Historians will rightly point out, however, that matters really didn't work out quite the way we as children are taught. Fact is, even after Lincoln signed the document, slavery was still legal in the five slave states not "in rebellion" and also in parts of the Confederacy under Union control in Virginia (including Norfolk and Portsmouth) and Louisiana (including New Orleans).

Almost three years later, in December of 1865, slavery at last did come to an end when the Thirteenth Amendment to the U.S. Constitution was ratified. Coming months after the Civil War ended, those words rather than the 1863 Emancipation Proclamation made slavery illegal everywhere in the United States.

Problem solved? Not by a long shot. California Institute of Technology Professor J. Morgan Kousser, who has published extensively on politics in the South after the Civil War, observes that:

"The U.S. was the only large slave society that quickly enfranchised ex-slaves [gave them the right to vote], and the eagerness and skill with which they [former slaves] took to politics surprised and dismayed their former masters, who had expected docility and incompetence.[13]

"Almost unanimously supporting the Republican party, the party of abolition [the end to slavery]…[former slaves as] freedmen elected governments that launched statewide education systems, encouraged railroads, passed civil rights laws, and protected the rights of laborers.

"Even after 1877 [and the end of the 12 years of "Reconstruction" after the Civil War], most black males retained the vote until suffrage restrictions adopted by Democratic legislatures and constitutional conventions in the years around 1900 disfranchised the vast majority of African-Americans and many poor whites.

"Social changes…also [had been] striking [during Reconstruction]. Blacks could legally marry, worship as they wished, form private clubs, receive (inferior) education at public expense, and often enjoy public accommodations such as restaurants, theaters, and railroads on a non-segregated basis…[if] they could afford to pay. Absolute segregation of public places arrived only towards the turn of the [20th] century, and it was a matter of law [so-called Jim Crow laws], not custom."

Relevant for our purposes in Kousser's writings is the *trust* everyone had that the former Confederate state governments meant exactly what they said about their *commitments* to strictly enforce Jim Crow laws. Everyone could *trust* that those commitments would be honored in full by the enforcers, using courts, jails and, if the enforcers felt the need, guns or nooses.

True, after the Thirteenth Amendment ending slavery was ratified late in 1865, Congress worked hard and fast to pass and ratify the Fourteenth Amendment, which became law in July 1868. In what was then thought to be crystal clear language, the Fourteenth Amendment to the Constitution gave definition to citizenship for blacks, due process protection for everyone, and equal rights under federal and state law.

Weren't these two constitutional amendments also the law that everybody else should have been trusting local authorities to enforce?

Not quite. During the 30 years after 1868, there was a fierce political and legal struggle to determine what the Fourteenth Amendment really meant, coupled with a massive effort in the former Confederate states to enact state laws that, practically speaking, eroded each and every right of black Americans that the Thirteenth and Fourteenth amendments in theory had guaranteed for all American citizens.

Worse still, everyone in the South knew there was good reason to trust in commitments made by local law enforcement to enforce those laws as they saw fit, not Washington—whether or not anyone else in any other part of the country liked what local Southern lawmen were saying...or doing.

Of course, at the time, a lot of Southern whites did like it, while most minorities did not, particularly black Americans, Jews, Catholics and other people of a different shade or religion who ended up lynched or beaten to death by all-white "all-American" mobs.

Racist state and local Southern government authorities and the Ku Klux Klan came to believe that they could act with impunity because, by the dawn of the Twentieth Century, they had the backing of a key federal institution: the then all-white, all-male bastion of American jurisprudence, the U.S. Supreme Court.

The U.S. Supreme Court? *Our* U.S. Supreme Court? How could that be?

Here's how. On May 8, 1896, 28 years after the Fourteenth Amendment was ratified, the Supreme Court made it crystal clear to everyone in the United States that, despite the precise wording of the Thirteenth and Fourteenth Amendments, states could resort to their own lawmaking to segregate blacks (or any other racially defined citizens for that matter) in just about any way and at any time they wished, and that they could do it as a matter of sound public policy.

What also became clear when this Supreme Court ruling issued forth from Washington was that everyone not only could *trust* in this decision, but that they could also *trust* local law enforcement's *commitment* to enforce it all over the South any way they chose.

This remarkable Supreme Court decision came down in a legal test case, *Plessy v. Ferguson*, which had been appealed over four years all the way from a local parish court in Louisiana. There, in New Orleans, with a good deal of citizen backing among blacks, Creoles and whites, Homer Plessy had purposefully gotten himself arrested on June 7, 1892, by boarding a whites-only railroad car.

Sitting there was prohibited by state law to anyone with even a trace of African heritage (Plessy was an "octoroon," someone of seven-eighths Caucasian and one-eighth African descent). Because of his heritage, under Louisiana law, Plessy was classified as black and was required to sit in the "colored" car.[14]

A local judge, John Howard Ferguson of the New Orleans Parish Court, had fined Plessy a then-not-insignificant sum of $25,[15] a judgment which Plessy and his backers purposefully appealed but lost again in a higher Louisiana court. However, that was precisely the outcome they wanted, for it opened the way for Plessy and his backers to take the dispute all the way to the U.S. Supreme Court.

Their goal? To secure a binding legal precedent in the form of a Supreme Court decision to overturn the Louisiana law as a violation of the Fourteenth Amendment. If they got what they wanted, the Court would effectively be barring racial discrimination nationwide, not just in Louisiana.

Alas, in what is today usually regarded as among the most tortured and repugnant decisions in the annals of Supreme Court history, seven sitting justices rejected Plessy's arguments. All the more remarkable, they did it, believe it or not, on the basis of the Fourteenth Amendment's very own wording!

The Court concluded that the Louisiana statute requiring blacks to sit in separate train cars in no way violated the Fourteenth Amendment. In doing so, the seven-justice Court majority actually rejected the view that the Louisiana law implied any inferiority of blacks that might otherwise be proscribed by the Amendment. Instead, it contended that the Louisiana law separated the two races as a matter of public policy, and that this policy sat just fine with the U.S. Supreme Court.[16]

Summarizing the majority opinion, Supreme Court Associate Justice Henry Billings Brown went on to declare: "We consider the underlying fallacy of the plaintiff's argument to consist in the assumption that the enforced separation of the two races stamps the colored race with a badge of inferiority. If this be so, it is not by reason of anything found in the [Fourteenth Amendment], but solely because the colored race chooses to put that construction upon it."

Appalled by the opinion that his colleagues were rendering, Justice John Marshall Harlan wrote a profoundly scathing and predictive dissent, insisting not only that the Court's decision was wrong, but also that the U.S. Constitution had to be considered as color-blind. Sadly, Harlan's logic was unhappily eye-opening when measured by modern-day legal and ethical standards. Wikipedia neatly sums up his painful-to-read logic this way:

> "Harlan highlighted the plight of blacks by pointing out that the Chinese, a race he viewed as inferior, could still ride with whites, '...a race so different from our own that we do not permit those belonging to it to become citizens of the United States. Persons belonging to it are, with few exceptions, absolutely excluded from our country,' he wrote."[17]

One could sum up Harlan's logic as centered on this idea: if we let those "inferior" Chinese in the door, why not blacks? Wikipedia continues:

> "The [Plessy] case helped cement the legal foundation for the *doctrine* of separate but equal, the idea that segregation based on [racial] classifications was legal as long as facilities were of equal quality. However, Southern state governments refused to provide blacks with genuinely equal facilities and resources in the years after the Plessy decision. The states not only separated races but, in actuality, ensured differences in quality."[18]

Let's focus on that word *doctrine*, which I purposefully italicized in the quote above.

A doctrine, oath, promise or even a law means absolutely nothing unless we *trust* that it will be enforced (think speed limits and parking meters!). We also have to trust that someone with the authority to do it will actually make that doctrine, law or promise stick (again, speed limits and parking meters).

More often than not, we love it when an institution keeps its promise or makes a law stick. Imagine, for example, that you have bought a lottery ticket for a $250,000,000 jackpot. The lottery publicly promises that if you pick the right numbers, you'll win. If you do win, you will absolutely love the fact that you trusted the lottery's promise to pay, not just the fact that you went out and bought the ticket.

In trusting the lottery's promise, you were really trusting in the *doctrine*—the policy—that the lottery had previously established, namely that it would do what it said, even though you could not prove at the moment you bought the ticket that they would actually do what they said they were going to do. Sure, you may have been aware of the lottery's past payouts, its promises to do just that, its doctrine that "We'll take a bit of your money now, but pay you a lot more if you win." Had you not *trusted* the lottery to do what it promised, you would have never bought the ticket in the first place.

Bottom line? Without your trust in others to do what they say they will, there can never be a commitment. Sure, there can be promises galore. Or vows, doctrines or laws, plus a lot of talk about deadlines and actions people will take. And you may sorely want to believe in all that, too. Ask anyone who's had to arduously negotiate with their insurance company and then wait forever for reimbursement after a big storm damaged their home. They'll tell you how much they first trusted their insurer—and why they'll be reluctant to again place blind faith—unquestioned trust—in the insurance company's future "commitments."

Not yet a believer that commitments require a goal, time, action *and* the trust that the one making a commitment will deliver the goods?

Try this front-page headline from the *New York Post* on Wednesday, June 27, 1990:

"Read My Lips! I Lied!"

Political junkies will recognize in an instant that the *Post* was referring to President George Herbert Walker Bush, who a day earlier had reneged on his most memorable headline-grabbing promise of the 1988 presidential campaign: "Read My Lips! No New Taxes!"

In breaking his campaign promise just two years after he made it, Bush was conceding to stark political, economic and federal budget reality. In 1990, the country was still reeling from the 1987 stock market crash. The U.S government deficit was out of control and growing faster than anyone had foreseen. By all accounts, even the heaviest federal budget cuts wouldn't help set things straight.

The prevailing wisdom on Capitol Hill and even on Wall Street was that Congress had to raise taxes, whether new or existing, not just cut federal spending. However, President Bush consistently resisted entreaties from both parties to go along. His message from the White House remained unchanged: "Read My Lips Again! No New Taxes!" Eventually, though, with the looming risk of an imminent government shutdown staring everyone in the face, Bush gave in, and by mid-1990, taxes went up.

Acid condemnation of Bush's alleged political treason immediately spewed forth from the political right, continuing nonstop. Two years later, during the 1992 presidential election campaign (which he lost to Bill Clinton), Bush felt compelled to offer up an abject apology, confessing that he should never have agreed to those higher taxes.

It was too late: Bush never recovered. And what was it that Bush could not recover from the most? Losing the trust of supporters and opponents alike that he would (so said his once-supporters) or even could (so said his opponents) deliver on his promises.

Worse for the folks who had once trusted Bush to deliver what they wanted, his supporters also had to accept their own mistake: that they should never have trusted him to deliver on his promises in the first place, and—worse—that they looked awfully dumb for having trusted him at all.

Bush lost big in the 1992 presidential election. His commitments—his promises to set certain goals, to contribute the time to make them happen, and to set actions in motion to achieve them— were rendered worthless as commitments once he had lost his supporters' trust. Even today, Bush's 1990 standout political fumbling remains potent fodder both for political satire and television's talking heads on the political left, in the center, and on the right.

Laughter is the best medicine, of course. Unfortunately, no one was laughing when another political commitment, made 48 years earlier than Bush's by two world leaders, melted away when one of them learned to his chagrin that his trust in the other was wholly misplaced.

I refer to Soviet dictator Josef Stalin, who in 1939 placed his complete trust in Adolf Hitler's agreement to ally Nazi Germany with the Soviet Union and, in the process, allow both the Soviet and Nazi governments to carve Central Europe into "spheres of influence", invade a few countries, and annex neighboring territories without fear of retaliation by the one against the other.

Historians have documented that for his part, Hitler placed little, if any, trust in the Soviet Union or its leadership. Instead, he was purposefully buying time to initiate and wrap up other military campaigns before unleashing Germany's massive military machine against the USSR. At the same time, he was importing from the Soviets as many raw materials as possible before firing the first salvo in Moscow's direction.

It was under these profoundly imbalanced circumstances that this "Treaty of Non-Aggression between Germany and the Soviet Union" was signed in the Kremlin in the late hours of August 23, 1939, by Stalin and Nazi Foreign Minister Joachim von Ribbentrop. The then-smiling Soviet leader never quite understood how he had been taken, or that a companion trade and economic pact agreed by the two countries just days before was in fact sought by Hitler solely to gain access to the very Soviet raw materials Berlin needed to further strengthen Germany's military capacity...

...to invade the Soviet Union itself!

Which is exactly what came to pass. On June 22, 1941, less than two years after the Nazi-Soviet pact was signed, Germany unleashed Operation Barbarossa, a wholesale invasion of the Soviet Union. Within a few weeks, the entirety of all territories gained by the Soviet Union under the original August 1939 treaty were reclaimed by Germany. Wikipedia's summary narrative is instructive as to what else happened:

> "Within six months, the Soviet military had
> suffered 4.3 million casualties and Germany had
> captured three million Soviet prisoners. The imports
> of Soviet raw materials into [and critical for]
> Germany over the duration of the two countries' [22-
> month-long] economic relationship proved vital to
> Operation Barbarossa. Without these Soviet imports,
> German stocks would have run out in several key
> products by October 1941, and Germany would have
> already run through its stocks of rubber and grain
> before the first day of the invasion."[19]

Though each would doubtlessly be loath to admit it today, President George Herbert Walker Bush's supporters (on the political right!) and Stalin himself (way to the political left!) actually shared one telling political tendency: placing their trust in someone who either was unable or unwilling to make his commitments stick. Either way, they lost.

What stings the most when it becomes crystal clear that you have misplaced your own trust? Well, haven't you ever heard someone ask: "How could you ever have trusted him?" At the core of this question is not what the other person did "wrong". Instead, it is what you did "wrong" by misplacing your trust in someone else.[20]

That stings a lot! Misery loves company, they say. So, if you would like some of that comfort right about now, rest assured that you are hardly alone in misplacing trust. People do it all the time. At the same time, don't be too comfortable, either, and instead ask yourself what most of those other people don't: how is it that we too often find out much too late exactly how and why we misplaced our trust?

The answer is simple if very hard to swallow: we let our hopes, dreams, and egos get in the way while deciding who deserves our trust.

Our hopes, our dreams, and certainly our egos will always weigh on our decision to trust someone else. They should. The issue is whether, before we actually declare our trust in other people who are to be part of the deal, we are realistically answering a heavy question: "How *much* am I letting my hopes, my dreams, and my ego blind me to how I might be trusting someone I shouldn't? How *might* I be placing my trust in someone who *can't* deliver no matter how much he or she wants to?"

Heavy questions indeed. And soon enough, we'll feel good about asking them.

Right now, remember only this: without real trust, no commitment ever exists, no matter what goals, time, and action you or anyone else brings to the table.

And unless that trust is well and wisely placed, not even the best goals, time and action plan will be enough for a commitment to work.

9. Trusting Ourselves to Ask for Help with Commitments

Blakely. What had I been giving him in return before that bitter moment unfolded that had made him now care so much about my fate?

What was his obligation to me that made him put his own life at greater risk than mine, much less the life of a nameless little kid whom I wanted to kill for stealing a few tools from a broken-down Army truck?

******

Why wouldn't Joe Blakely let me shoot the boy?

I was screaming bloody murderous hatred. Frozen in place, Blakely gasped open-mouthed, unbelieving as I lifted the M-16 to wipe that little bastard running away from us right off the face of the earth. Blakely lunged toward the deadly dark of the rifle barrel as the power of death drew my finger to the trigger.

It might as well have been the voice of God. "Don't!" he shouted.

1968, near Bien Hoa, Vietnam, left, Joe Blakely, right, the author

Blakely won the race. But whose life did he save that day? The child's? Or mine? Had my E-5 sergeant not bet his life against the muzzle of my rifle, wouldn't the rage that drove me so close to destroying that kid have haunted me every day since? Wouldn't that acid have eaten away my being? Wouldn't it have left me and maybe others among the living dead, a victim of corrosive anger that would forever leave me scarred beneath my veneer of civility?

Welcome to what was our war in Vietnam: an unending, dirty, dusty, dank, hot, humid vortex sucking me and millions of others into a battle that should never have been waged. God-awful mess that I knew it was, I still couldn't quell my seething fury over the taunting anonymity of that child thief. Instead, I was raging inside yet again at being mired in the futility of our country's fool's errand that year, that month, that day, that minute.

Now that Joe had made sure I couldn't pull the trigger anymore, all I had left was that soul-searing resentment over the indifference of these tens of thousands of people teeming in Saigon's streets that May 1968 day, a day when our sergeant major had been so horribly slaughtered. It had long ago become so easy for me to rationalize my bitterness! After all, not a one of these people cared a bit that Sergeant Major K or any of us were there, right? All they could do, day in and day out, was to stare at us strangers in a strange land, dust-covered and decked out head to foot in the green grey tan that marked us more as suckers, not soldiers.

Yet they to whom this land really belonged and we who had no legitimate claim to anything here sure did have one thing in common that day: we were all part of a pathetic tidal wave of human traffic clogging that broken-down city's arteries, running either to escape death or fight it...moving as fast as the narrow streets would allow.

Why did Blakely save me? What had I been giving him in return before that bitter moment unfolded that had made him now care so much about my fate? What was my sergeant's obligation to me that made him put his own life at greater risk than mine, much less the life of a nameless little kid whom I wanted to kill for stealing a few tools from a broken-down Army truck?

For that matter, what was Joe's commitment to me? When had I agreed to it? What was I giving him in return?

And what help had I asked of him or anyone else to make it all work?

People who fly into a rage always make a bad landing.

Will Rogers

Few things help an individual more than to place responsibility upon him, and to let him know that you trust him.

Booker T. Washington

Piglet sidled up to Pooh from behind. "Pooh!" he whispered. "Yes, Piglet?" "Nothing," said Piglet, taking Pooh's paw. "I just wanted to be sure of you."

A.A. Milne, Winnie The Pooh

It is said that every snowflake...

... is unique. While that may be true, at their core, they are really all the same: plain old frozen water. The same can be said for commitments. They may seem as unique as snowflakes, but at their core, they are really all made up of the same core elements.

That hardly explains *why* we make commitments. The answer to that question lies in a certain reality of life: left to our own devices, we'll never get what we want. Others must be involved. Thus it is that through the ages, people have relied on commitments to and from others for getting just about anything they want, mixing together goals, time, actions and trust that everyone will do his or her part to make it all work.

Not to be overlooked: those other folks in the deal have to trust us as much as we trust them. No one can ever make a valid commitment *to* you to do something *for* you unless that person trusts you to do something you've promised to do in return. Alas, because we can never prove in advance that we will succeed in meeting our part of any commitment to them, we can never know for sure that we will keep the trust of those very people who are counting on us.

How do we solve this problem? By recognizing that earning, nourishing, and keeping the trust of others is a non-stop task. It requires that you always be up front with them about the limits of your power to deliver what you promise, and that you will always be ready to ask for help in delivering on your part of the deal whenever it is obvious that you need that help.

Unless you acknowledge your limits and the companion willingness to ask for help when you need it, the people whose trust you want and need to keep will be unable to trust you even if they want to.

Here's a poignant example. After suffering and then recovering from two debilitating and nearly fatal strokes in her early fifties, Alison Bonds Shapiro authored *Healing Into Possibility*,[21] a frank and rigorous personal account of the rough emotional sledding she faced while struggling to get back on her feet. In her book, she writes:

> "If we want to trust someone else, we begin with
> first learning who we are, what we want and what
> we know about ourselves as we grow and change.
> We explore our strengths, boundaries and
> limitations. Knowing who we are and what we are
> capable of, we learn how to trust ourselves."

Shapiro goes further. People usually do not take the time, she observes, to assess their personal strengths and weaknesses until something awful happens to them. Only in the face of that major personal challenge do we begin to understand that "we have not looked as closely as we might."

Then, in a line of thought paralleling why I believe some people ask for God's help in making good on a promise, vow, or commitment while others of us turn to friends, advisors or books, Shapiro sets down how people can find their way back to that essential trust in themselves, or perhaps find it for the first time:

> "[So] now we [start to] ask: How do I get things
> done? What are my strengths and limitations? How
> do my strengths work with my unique movement
> patterns? How will I negotiate around my
> limitations?"

Shapiro was referring to how hard it was after her stroke to move physically, and to do the things that once came so easily. Her prescription also confirms that we absolutely need the trust—and help—of someone else and probably many others besides to honor a commitment we have made to someone else.

To win that trust and the companion access to that help, we first need to show that we trust ourselves enough to do what we promise, and that we know enough about our own limits that might make it harder, not easier, to deliver on the promise. Knowing our own limits is the only way to ask for and get the right help from the right people at the right time for getting the right job done.

Shapiro also identifies how asking others to help you deliver on a commitment to them helps build their trust in you:

> "Building trust in ourselves requires us first to look closely at ourselves, being honest about what we discover. Then we must practice compassion for and acceptance of the person we are discovering ourselves to be. Being willing to know is not the same as harshly judging. Harsh judgments close us off to ourselves. Compassion, forgiveness and acceptance open us up and allow us to learn."

That includes learning what help we may need and whom to ask for that help. "As we experience relationships," Shapiro goes on to observe,

> "… we come to realize that in a relationship, two people never fully know one another or can expect that the other person will do exactly what we want…particularly if we ourselves are not certain what we want and need or how to ask for it."

Shapiro's astute reasoning points directly to something so obvious about commitments that it invariably stays hidden in plain sight from most of us: commitments always confirm relationships, whether between you and yourself (a self-commitment) or between you and at least one other. Relationships also happen to be the "stuff" and structure of help and of asking for help, which makes relationships the "stuff" of commitments, too.

Why, then, does it seem as if the harder we work to earn and keep trust, and the better we get at asking for help when we need it, the potential remains so high that the commitment still will fail?

COMMITMENTS

10. Why Most Commitments Don't Work the Way We Planned (or at all!)

Perhaps it was my own anger and frustration, after finding out that Buddy's apocryphal story was actual fact—the one about his having saved the Laggin' Dragon, a World War II B-29 that just happened to be carrying one of the atomic bombs across the Pacific to drop on Nagasaki.

How could we have been so deafly arrogant for failing to hear and then accept the truth much earlier than we did, in enough time to do some good?

I'm still stung by the memory of that November 2006 trip up to New York to take him back down to Washington, so he could stand alongside the newly restored Enola Gay and receive Air Force and Smithsonian recognition, 62 years too late, for his job well-done.

******

It was no secret anymore that Uncle Buddy had been starving himself to death. Long ago resigned to the hapless fate of outliving his wife, his friends and even his latest rescue dog, my late mother's brother had decided to escape his prison of abject loneliness once and for all.

Once every couple of weeks, I would assault his fierce independent streak by making the 550-mile round trip by car from Washington, DC, to New York City to get him out of the house.

Maybe I'd take him to Costco for hearing aid batteries or groceries he'd never eat, or to the Woodro deli[22] in Hewlett for a decent meal, just to get him on his feet and moving around a bit. "C'mon, Buddy, it'll be good for you," I kept insisting.

That was then. Now? It was E reminding me. "Wait," she called out, "don't forget the Jim Beam!" I turned back as the others walked towards their cars, watched as she poured a little into a plastic cup, tipped it, and let the bourbon gently fall over his casket. I followed her lead in toasting Buddy and saying our last farewells. The tears that came to E's eyes were the most genuine of any flowing that April morning. And she wasn't even family. Just a friend. My dear friend. My beloved.

It hadn't been that many days before when Buddy had been holding my hand tightly, surprising me with his strength. He was lying in bed, curled fetus-like, a mere shadow of his former robust self. Without the slightest murmur, he signaled to me that he knew I was there. I want you to know how much I love you, he seemed to want to whisper from his silence, but now, Cliff, would you please just let me die?

Pretty please?

No matter that we had worked so hard to guarantee the twice-daily plasticized airline-style Meals-On-Wheels as proof that he'd not go hungry. How could we have known that those trays would instead become for him a ghastly checkered flag: "The race of life is over, David Klein, you've done well, but you can't cook for yourself anymore, and you can't drive anywhere anymore, and your friends are all dead and buried, so now it's your turn to get off the track and leave the field to others."

In the decades before, we had never been really that close, Buddy and me. His bizarre, demented wife Yetta, whom none of the extended family ever really liked and who surely didn't like us, had become a clandestine barrier to anyone's getting past a thin veneer of laughter and joke-telling that perennially marked Buddy's banter at Thanksgiving or Hanukkah family dinners, all while she just sat there, brooding silently.[23]

No, Buddy and his very strange wife were in a world of their own, drawn away from his blood relatives by Yetta's DNA of seething hatred of us for crimes never defined.

Only after she died did Buddy confess to how strongly Yetta despised us, and to his own self-resentment for having succumbed to her caustic threats to make his life even more miserable if he reached out to us in genuine friendship.

Why, suddenly, had I begun to care about him so much? Was it my own peculiar ego trip, a quest to garner praise from the rest of the family? "Geez, Cliff, what a great guy you are for doing all this for Buddy."

Perhaps it was my own anger and frustration, after finding out that Buddy's apocryphal story was actual fact—the one about his having saved the Laggin' Dragon, a World War II B-29 that just happened to be carrying one of the atomic bombs across the Pacific to drop on Nagasaki.

How could we have been so deafly arrogant for failing to hear and then accept the truth much earlier than we did, in enough time to do some good?

I'm still stung by the memory of that November 2006 trip up to New York to take him back down to Washington so he could stand alongside the newly restored Enola Gay—and receive Air Force and Smithsonian recognition, 62 years too late, for his job well-done.

David Klein, our "Uncle Buddy" at his WW II barracks at Mather Field near Sacramento, California, Spring, 1945

Captain Edward M. Costello. (Airplane Commander)
Top row, l to r—Captain Edward M. Costello, 2nd Lt. Harry B. Davis, 2nd Lt. Robert J. Petrolli, 2nd Lt. Thomas H. Brumagin, 2nd Lt. John L. Downey.
Middle row, l to r—Cpl. James R. Bryant, M/Sgt. Carleton A. McEachern, Sgt. Maurice J. Clark, Sgt. David Purdon.
Bottom row, l to r—Pfc. James W. McGlennon, Sgt. Robert E. Holse, S/Sgt. Robert J. Dowling, Pfc. Fred D. Butler, Cpl. Robert R. Garn, Pfc. Charles W. Rich, M/Sgt. John C. Hansen.

*The crew of the Laggin' Dragon, June, 1945, after
the atomic bomb had been dropped on Nagasaki*

Was I appointing myself team leader for all of us Brody children, and all of Buddy's nephews and nieces, who were now pitching in to get to know their 83-year-old uncle probably for the very first time? I just don't know.

Is an uncle's love strong enough on its own to suffice as the payback for the commitment that I and my siblings and cousins were now making to help sustain Buddy's existence?

Were his gentle words of gratitude enough of a return on investment for my commitment to traipse up there time after time? Was I really helping him, as he said I was, in dealing with the sadness that he no longer had enough time to get to know his nephews and nieces the way he still wanted? Oh, if only Yetta had not been around, he cried. We cried...

Why did I do all these things? Am I so heroically selfless? Or is it the height of selfishness that drove me to make these "sacrifices" when the truth is that all I wanted was to lay claim to glory and prod others to tell me what a great guy I am?

Damn! E is so very right, so very smart.

"Stop wearing yourself out with all these dumb questions about commitment and just do what Buddy would have done—have another shot of Jimmy Bee."

She's got that right!

The human story does not always unfold like a
mathematical calculation on the principle that two and
two make four. Sometimes in life they make five or
minus three; and sometimes the blackboard topples
down in the middle of the sum and leaves the class in
disorder and the pedagogue with a black eye.

Winston Churchill

Lots of people want to ride with you in the limo, but
what you want is someone who will take the bus with
you when the limo breaks down.

Oprah Winfrey

You have a good heart and you think the good
thing is to be guilty and kind but it's not always kind to
be gentle and soft. There's a genuine violence [that]
softness and kindness visit on people. Sometimes self-
interested is the most generous thing you can be.

Tony Kushner

Your conscience is the measure of the honesty of
your selfishness. Listen to it carefully.

Richard Bach

For commitments to work, we must...

...trust other people enough to ask for their help when we need it, because we cannot get anything done without them and without their help. That, in turn, requires them to trust us to pull our share of the load. Our pulling that load is a major part of the "price" we'll pay for their trusting us in the first place, and certainly for giving us their help when we need it.

We also know from life experience that a lot of commitments in which we've been involved have failed, and that we've felt awful whenever that happened. Or awfully stupid. Yet, after all that special pain, we make even more commitments.

Why do we do it? The answer is simple: to avoid even worse pain if we instead just sit on our hands or wall ourselves off from the world.

Why else, for example, would we pay income taxes? Why else would we go to the dentist? (Ugh!) Or wait for hours at the DMV for a license or car inspection? Or go off to Vietnam, Iraq, or Afghanistan and risk being killed in action? Yes, women and men in military service may indeed want to serve their country, but it is the rare soldier, sailor, airman, or marine out there who wants to be killed doing it. I never met any.

If by making a commitment we're fated to a Hobson's Choice[24] — doing something we don't like just because the alternative is worse — why would we ever make a commitment, no less accept someone's else's commitment, if it is also true that most commitments never quite work out the way they were meant? History and human nature predict that even after we take on the hard parts of honoring a commitment, it is not likely to work exactly as hoped or maybe not at all.

Isn't there a better way?

Actually, there isn't. And not just because, in today's litigious society, a commitment in hand, especially a written one, makes it easier to sue someone who doesn't do something promised.

The truth is, we have to make commitments to get anything done. Anything! Even if it means lots of Hobson's Choices later on down the road.

Remember Henry VIII? He made one commitment after another not just because he had to or even wanted to. Instead, it was clear that to get something he wanted from the someone he wanted it from, he had to agree to give that someone something in return.

There is more. The people to whom you make your promise to deliver, and whom you have also convinced to trust you to deliver the goods, must place *value* on whatever it is that you're going to deliver to them. This applies even for Mother Theresa and all like her who have given so much and so completely of themselves. These nominally selfless people have always demanded something very specific in exchange for what they were giving, are giving, and will be giving tomorrow.

More later about what selfless people want in return. Right now, I'll bet those of you who practice law may already be thinking "contracts." Contract law centers on one concept: two parties agreeing to an exchange of values. "I'll give you this, if you give me that." That's why contracts usually start with words like "in consideration of."

That word, *consideration*, has nothing to do with how nice people are being to each other. Rather, it conveys a centuries-old idea: that something of value given by one person to another is in consideration of (the taking into account of) the second person handing back something of equal value.

Usually that consideration is money. The fiver that you hand to the barista at Starbucks is literally the consideration you are providing in exchange for the coffee drink you're getting.

Moreover, you make that exchange because, believe it or not, you are explicitly agreeing that the value of the latte is exactly worth the price Starbucks sets out in writing on the menu board. Maybe you thought the barista's concoction was pricey. But unless someone was forcing you at gunpoint to hand over the money against your will, you agreed at the very moment you forked over the dough that the exchange of values—your dollars for their latte—was exactly what it should be.

By contrast, when we make a vow or promise, or even take an oath, there does not have to be an exchange of values—no consideration at all. There may be consideration, but when I promise to drive more carefully or to be there at eight in the morning and then slow down at the wheel or actually show up on time, there has been no exchange of values promised, no consideration at all.[25]

This brings us to the heart of why commitments are a world apart from promises, vows and oaths.

As imperfect or unworkable as commitments may end up being, we make them because there is no other way we can ever hope to get back something of value equal to what we are giving in exchange.

Remember that latte? It is obvious that dollar bills are not coffee, right? But no one ever said that they were the same thing. Instead, despite their obvious physical differences, the barista and the customer agreed that these two radically different things were of exact equal value in the eyes of Starbucks and me, the customer.

However, if we're saying that what counts is the equality of value rather than whether the things being exchanged are identical, we're also saying something else critical to how commitments work or not: value, like beauty, is in the eyes of the beholder.

Here's a great example of what this means. My sweetheart thinks I am out of my mind paying almost five dollars for a Starbucks latte.

She's a 7-Eleven coffee woman if there ever was one. She's also quite happy at the McCafe or Sheetz[26] coffee bar. In the process, she spends half of what I do for coffee and, son of a gun, I can't argue with what she thinks both beauty and value are: those coffees she buys not only look good and taste good but also cost a whole lot less!

The fact is that my sweetheart is not prepared to give Starbucks anywhere near the "consideration" I am for its coffee, because she believes that the value they assign to their lattes is way above the value she assigns to them. As a result, there is no commitment between her and Starbucks, no deal to exchange anything, and, I have to admit, more money left over in her pocket than mine.

If value, like beauty, is in the eyes of the beholder, and if people will always debate the dollar value of tangibles like coffee, cars, restaurant meals and airfares, what happens when the proposed commitment centers on something less tangible?

Like loving, honoring and cherishing?

Some of you may already be thinking: "If the people getting married are promising the same thing to one another—that is, to love, honor and cherish each other—isn't that 'fair consideration', that equal value we have been talking about?" You might go even farther and insist: "They're exchanging the same exact thing!"

Are they? I pose this question now because the same words, even the same sounds, can mean profoundly different things to different people. Woe unto you if you believe otherwise.

True story time.

Years ago, two small towns in Europe, one in France and the other in England, were twinned. That is, in a practice common all over Europe and increasingly among U.S. cities and their counterparts in other countries, these two towns became social and civic partners out of genuine friendship. They celebrated holidays, arranged student exchanges, and sponsored joint cultural programs every year. Better still, in alternating years, each town was host to hundreds of visitors from the other, honoring them with music and dancing in the streets until the wee hours. The local shopkeepers loved it, too, since they rang up lots of new business.

One year, when it was the Brits' turn to receive the visitors from France, the local village council decided that in honor of the soon-to-be arriving French, all the village shops would run special sales, aggressively lowering their prices. To be even more clever about it, council members decided that large banners promoting the discounts should be draped in each store window on High Street, the town's main thoroughfare.

But how should these banners read? One bright light suggested that the campaign be branded: "French Sales." Not too charmed by the sight or sound of that wording, someone else suggested: why not use French grammar, in which the adjective *French* would come after the word *Sales* and, even better, write *French* in, you guessed it, French!

The vote "yes" was immediate and unanimous! So it was that over a hundred banners, two feet tall, nine feet long, were printed up and taped in the front windows of every store on High Street, each proudly proclaiming in the red, white and blue national colors of both countries:

!!! Sales Français!!!

Neat, huh? At least the Brits thought so. Alas, not the French: "Sales Français" means "You Dirty Frenchman!" back there in Paris. And in the rest of the French-speaking world, too!

The moral of this story?

The risk is high that the words you speak will not be heard, much less understood, exactly the way you meant. The fact that this risk is so high is compelling proof in and of itself that the road to hell really can be paved with good intentions—especially when it comes to commitments involving anything intangible.

Worse still, the words you read or hear may mean something radically different to the speaker than to you or to your intended spouse especially when the subject at hand is loving, honoring, and cherishing rather than something more tangible and short-lived. Even when you write the words down, the potential for catastrophe is high, as our British friends quickly discovered.

Unless, that is, everyone who takes part in the deal—the commitment—also takes the time before they sign on to ask one another what they each think the commitment means, where they think misunderstandings might arise, and—rather than trying to guess at and write down every last one—how they'll go about trying to resolve them when they pop up.[27]

Unhappily, even after doing all this, there is still no guarantee for successfully getting past future hurdles. It only ensures that trying to get past these obstacles will be easier. Achieving this result will hardly be easy, either. When all is said and done, no one can predict what the future may bring.

For example: John and I commit (in writing, even!) to a partnership in which he will use his rocket science expertise to assemble and launch a spaceship, and I will supply the money for him to bring together the people and things he needs to make it all happen. A week later, John is killed in a car accident. Did he break his commitment? Should I sue his estate? Doubtful.

The point is: if it is much harder to be sure of what commitments mean when the proposed exchange is for intangible things (love, honor, cherish) rather than tangible ones like money and coffee, John's tragic death confirms something equally as problematic: all commitments include one particular intangible that tops all others— the future. Not knowing what the future portends explains simply and completely why most commitments don't work the way we originally thought they would.

Whew! We sure do seem to be stuck with a lot of inescapable Hobson's Choices, and a bunch of intangibles, too.

- We know from our own experience that commitments usually don't work out exactly the way we expected.

– We know that oftentimes, they don't work at all.

– We know that we are always hurting when they don't work.

– We know that after they don't work, we will almost always go out and make even more commitments.

– We know that we'll do this because there is no other way, that is, if we want something in return for what we offer to give in exchange.

– We know that in many of these exchanges, the things of equal value being exchanged are entirely intangible.

– Last and certainly not least, we know that in all commitments, at least one thing being worked into the deal is both intangible and, worse, unpredictable: the future.

This is the case even regarding Mother Theresa, who needed other people to accept her helping hand in exchange for the "something" she really wanted *from* them: a wholly intangible yet undeniably real sense of deep personal self-satisfaction and inner peace.

This demand for deep personal satisfaction drives all of us, even people who wall themselves off from the rest of humanity for hours, days, weeks, or even longer and commit to paint, write, compose, create or even garden all by themselves.

In those types of commitments, the deals we make are with ourselves: committing to do something that will make us feel happy with ourselves. But even when the deal is between me and myself, I cannot possibly know for sure how it will all turn out.

Why, with our eyes wide open, do we willingly take on all these unpredictable uncertainties of what the future may hold? It is not because we are masochistic. Instead, it is because we know deep down that like it or not, to get what we want, we have to accept that we can never know in advance whether we'll be successful holding someone else's feet to the fire, much less our own.

The only way to find out whether we actually can hold someone's feet to the fire—even our own—is by entering into a commitment.

A few chapters ago, I asked you to tuck the phrase "emotionally impelled" in the back of your mind? It is now time to resurrect it and confirm how it fits here.

Whenever we are faced with uncertainties, like what the future may have in store, we are emotionally impelled to seek out as much predictability as possible from the people and world around us. This helps us soften that searing pain of not knowing what the future has in store.

As a structured approach to dealing with the future, commitments are a profoundly effective remedy to lessen that searing pain of the unknown. They offer us at least some security when we cannot be perfectly secure. They provide some control when we cannot control everything. And, they give us a hold, albeit imperfect, on how the future might unfold if we work hard at it.

Think of it this way: commitments offer us every opportunity to make our own luck in getting what we want, and to squeeze out as much uncertainty as we can, even though we cannot squeeze out all uncertainty, no less predict the future or know in advance that the commitment will work. And we'll make the next commitment, and the next one after that, even after earlier ones fail, for these very reasons.

There are a couple of more reasons we'll do that, too. And they're good news!

COMMITMENTS

11. Successful Commitments: Two Secret Sauces

"This is neither the time nor place for that conversation," she shot back.

I looked at her as hard as she was staring at me. "Maybe not, but you have far less time than you think to decide when and where the time is right, and you are running out of that time much faster than you think. Sooner, not later. That's the only option you have."

Her jaw dropped. She said nothing, but for the first time in so many years, instead of the hardness, there was an unmistakable look of realization on her face. She had never thought of that, it seemed to me. Her hand covered her mouth as I turned and walked away.

******

How could I keep the trust of someone dear to me whose trust I had lost when our lives had changed so much for the worse? Or had my daughter never really trusted me in the first place? Had I been deluding myself by assuming all along that because she was my child, her trust in me was a given?

Years had gone by since the 2005 divorce, and there was still no warmth between us. One could easily say that my daughter and I were estranged, but that is too fancy a way to put it. She was determined not to give me the time of day, and that was that! On the few occasions when we were in the same room, she went out of her way to make sure the distance between us was the greatest that space would allow.

And no words, just a hard, stone-cold stare.

How could I repair this damage? Was it even possible? If not, what did that say about the value of my ideas, the ones I had so confidently preached during her first 16 years, that people should and could get along, no matter how tough the going? That was then and this was now: had I really know anything about building her confidence that teaming with me on anything was worth her while? Not much, it seemed.

Nor did it seem to make any difference to her that I still wanted to deliver on being a good father—whatever that meant. How else could I keep her trust, I wondered. And what was driving my need for reconciliation? Her welfare? Mine? Or was I simply trying to escape the pain of my daughter's rejection? Or worse still, was I just feeding my own ego?

"Keep at it, Cliff, and be patient," friends would say, sharing compelling lessons learned from their own less-than-happy family dynamics. I kept asking myself: keep at what? Sending her a birthday card each year wasn't going to magically open any doors to a warm and cuddly father-daughter relationship. My daughter was never the warm and cuddly type to start with!

I sent the cards anyway. Whether that put me on the right side of God or anyone else, I don't know. I simply kept on agreeing with anyone who counseled me to be flexible and "give it time."

Give it time? The truth is, I couldn't stand the condescension woven into the let's-talk-about-something-else fabric of those words.

Indeed, the moment finally came when I had heard that sweet talk one too many times: "I don't have that much time left," I snapped back. "Unless she gets run over by a bus, my daughter will have a lot more time on this earth to make up with me, but at this pace, it'll be long after I'm dead and buried when she finally gets around to doing it." If ever, I added in the privacy of my inner thoughts.

What a simple truth. And like so many other simple truths, it had been staring me in the face all along, hiding in plain sight, stark in its black-and-white clarity: I didn't have anywhere near the time everyone said it might take to wait for fate to put humpty-dumpty back together. There was a companion truth: the wrong people were hearing about who had what time left, while the most important person in the mix—along with me—was seemingly ignorant of how time was slipping away, never to be made up.

Taking advantage of our being at the same place at the same time in the same room at my son's wedding late in 2012, I said to my daughter that our getting together to sort things out was something for the here-and-now, not for an indeterminate date in an ill-defined future.

"This is neither the time nor place for that conversation," she shot back.

I looked at her as hard as she was staring at me. "Maybe not, but you have far less time than you think to decide when and where the time is right, and you are running out of that time much faster than you think. Sooner, not later. That's the only option you have."

Her jaw dropped. She said nothing, but for the first time in so many years, instead of the hardness, there was an unmistakable look of realization on her face. She had never thought of that, it seemed to me. Her hand covered her mouth as I turned and walked away.

And then?

The actual aisle at the Safeway supermarket where I was searching so hard for one value but found something far more worthwhile. Those are Progresso soups at the top left. On sale...

Well, it is already well into 2013. Spring has come, at least by the calendar, but here in Washington, we are being driven crazy by yet another cold, grey day in a winter that just won't quit. I'm in the Safeway to buy more of that canned soup still on sale, looking down at the shelf by the floor to make sure that I pick the "Rich and Hearty" Progresso label and not the "Traditional" style so that I don't lose that dollar-per-can discount. What is it with me and Progresso soups on sale, anyway?

"Hi Dad!"

There she is, walking in my direction. "How're you doing?"

The reason a lot of people do not recognize opportunity is because it usually goes around wearing overalls looking like hard work.

Thomas A. Edison

"I had a daddy, didn't I? He wasn't perfect and he certainly wasn't the one I'd dreamed he would have been, but I had one all the same. And I'd loved him as much as I'd hated him, hadn't I? All that distance, all that time wasted, but the fact that he'd inspired such passion in me meant something in itself. I can honestly say now that I think that's special. Screwed up and turned inside out, we were special him and me, and I am so thankful that I can say that I had a daddy and that he mattered. All his faults and failures mean nothing to me now."

Melodie Ramone, After Forever Ends

I could tell that my parents hated me. My bath toys were a toaster and a radio.

Rodney Dangerfield

The most loving parents and relatives commit murder with smiles on their faces. They force us to destroy the person we really are: a subtle kind of murder.

Jim Morrison

So, we've discovered, we have no...

...choice except to make more commitments after earlier commitments fail, that is, if we're ever to get what we want. But there must be a way to make at least a few of them work, right?

And if so, what is the secret sauce in successful commitments that broken ones don't have?

A gymnast from Virginia Beach, Virginia, may have answered that question for us.

Remember Gabby Douglas' huge smile at the 2012 London Olympics? She was deservedly pleased not just with her own performance but also with her team's stellar gold medal gymnastics wins. We all were!

Even more telling were the thoughts Douglas shared days later during an interview with *Vanity Fair* magazine. Disclosing a lot about what drives this extraordinary athlete, her words also revealed the first of two secret sauces in successful commitments.

Vanity Fair's Buzz Bissinger had asked Douglas about all that post-Olympic fame she was enjoying: "How do you feel about all the attention?" he prodded. "Is it weird? Is it strange?"

Her response? "I love all the attention, people noticing me. 'There's the gymnast! There she is!' "[28]

And that is exactly what we all want from a commitment: recognition.

You wouldn't be faulted for thinking that I'm referring to recognition for a job well done. Douglas surely deserved tremendous recognition for that, as her gold medal so eloquently confirms. But that recognition came only after she delivered, not before.

At issue here is a completely different form of recognition, namely your recognition of the risk someone else is taking by trusting you—when first entering into the commitment with you—that you eventually *will* deliver what you say you will.

Say what? You must prove somehow that you understand someone else's risk? "What about my risk?" you may argue.

Yes, you are taking a risk, too, and we'll get to your risk soon enough. Right now, though, focus where most people never do, namely on the other person's betting on you. Along with meeting goals, giving your time, taking actions, delivering the goods, trusting someone else, giving others reason to trust you, and making sure the goods you are delivering equal the value that someone else is giving you in exchange, you must explicitly acknowledge the risk other people are taking in the deal—their risk in trusting you at the beginning of the commitment, not just later on down the road.

Acknowledging that risk is the first "secret sauce" of successful commitments.

Is it really possible in advance and during the lifetime of a commitment to prove convincingly that you are consistently sensitive to the risk someone else is taking by trusting you?

Alas, it isn't possible. As eloquent and compelling as they might be, your spoken or written words meant to create or sustain that feeling of trust can always be changed simply by replacing what you said or wrote yesterday with something that you say or write today.

The same holds true even for most of your actions. Very few deeds are immutable or unchangeable, apart from those with precise, finite outcomes like driving into a ditch or breaking the bat after hitting a curve ball out of the park.

Since most of your actions in a commitment are a part of a Work In Progress, their impact can be modified and sometimes even undone, either by unwinding the action or by taking some other action that, intentionally or not, sweeps the effect of the first go-round off the table.

How? I send you a check but stop payment on it. I change the oil but forget to tighten the oil filter cap, all the oil leaks out by week's end, and you can't drive anywhere. A U.S. presidential candidate swears there will be no new taxes and then approves legislation raising tax rates. A German chancellor signs a nonaggression pact with another country and then invades it. A sweet couple from Keokuk, Iowa, marries then divorces. The list goes on and on.

If I can't prove what I must prove—that someone will be better off accepting the risk of trusting me—is there anything at all that I can do about this?

Yes. Declaring at the very beginning of every commitment that you will be flexible during the life of any commitment, *meaning it when you say it*, and then being ready to help figure out whether and how everyone might bend with the winds of change if those winds call for changing the nature of the commitment during its lifetime.

How many Jews, alive at the time of the Holocaust, swore that they would never speak to another German, only to have eventually made a troubled peace with that past and visited Germany? Many. Some have even chosen to live there. Talk about flexibility. How many people, after losing loved ones in horrible crimes, have wished death upon the perpetrators but then made a troubled peace with their loss and even forgiven (if not forgotten) the wrongdoers' actions? A lot.

How many parents, having "lost it" with a seemingly errant child, almost immediately recognized that there was a better way of dealing with it? How many have pulled back on a threatened punishment, especially after calm returned and it looked like the children might have been on solid ground after all? No parent I ever knew, including the one I see in the mirror every day, ever liked having to eat that crow, but the ones who were flexible enough to do it are glad they did.

Can everyone scarred by awful personal experiences like the Holocaust or the murder of a loved one reassess their feelings like this? Can everyone bend with such strong winds of change? Not by a long shot. If even a few can, especially when the personal and emotional stakes can be so high, then the rest of us ought to be able to bend with lesser winds of change if that's what is needed. And the truth is that to keep most commitments alive, the winds of change will be much lighter and require much less bending!

How does bending with the winds of change relate to recognizing someone else's risk of trusting in you and in the commitments you make?

Here's how. During the life of any commitment, especially when unexpected or unwelcome surprises make things look doubtful, you will have opportunities to say and do things consistent with the other person's expectations that you *still* want to deliver the goods. That's what the bending is all about.

Bending with the wind every time it blows is the second secret sauce in all successful commitments. Not only does it serve to sustain others' trust in you, but it also opens the way for re-establishing that trust later on down the road when problems arise.

Flexibility on your part will require adjusting what you say and do about the commitment, maybe even eating some of that crow I was just talking about. It may also include working hard with the person whose trust you want to keep, to modify the original deal, or to replace it wholesale so that the final product fits with today's new reality.

To repeat: stating openly and explicitly at the outset of any commitment that you will be flexible *during the lifetime of the commitment* helps immeasurably to gain the other person's trust, and to keep it when the going gets tough.

If confirming that you'll bend with the wind mitigates the other person's risk, saying you'll do it is rarely easy and in truth will usually be very hard. Keeping your word as events unfold later on will be even harder. And if the only other option is ending the commitment before it has succeeded—and that *is* the only other option—then it is either saying you'll make changes when the need arises and then actually doing it, or giving up.

This second secret sauce of commitments, showing genuine flexibility when confronted by problems meeting the commitment, actually does two magical things for you: not only conveying that you understand the other person's risk, but also reducing your own risk in trusting the other person!

Remember? At the very point when I first talked about the other person's risk, you shot back: "What about my risk?" You solve the problem of your own risk-taking by demanding from the others that they give you the very same value you are giving them: flexibility when dealing with changes. It is as simple as that.

Just be prepared to match your words with that action when the time comes—which it will—if you want a commitment with real potential to make everyone happy with the outcome.

12. Commitments That Work: The Last Two (Not-So-Secret) Ingredients

I wasn't prepared for what came next. As I was staring down at the street, his next comment hit me harder than my teammate back in Little League who, without meaning to do it, whacked me on the side of my head with his baseball bat.

"You know, Cliff, it's tough out there..."

As his toxic message burned my ears and my soul, a big truck slowly made its way around the parked cars on C Street seven stories below us. It had that huge, baby blue logo marking a truck leasing company that all of us here in the Baltimore-Washington metro area know for its sparklingly clean white vehicles: "Brody Truck Rental."

"Go to hell, Harry. If *that* Brody can make it 'out there' by renting trucks, I ought to be able to do something worth something to someone 'out there,' too!"

But did I really say that to Harry?

******

He had been my political *and* policy enemy, much higher than me on the State Department totem pole back then and certainly now. Yet I had beaten him back. I went around him, behind him, below him, all the way to the president, just to get my way. Screw the chain of command. I had been hell bent for leather to beat this guy at his own game. And I did.

That was then, more than three years before, and this was now. The tables were turned, weren't they, with the future of my diplomatic career now totally in *his* hands. Well, I had relished in my victory, so who could blame him for thinking now that his revenge would be so sweet.

On and on he went about the virtues of being a "respected" U.S. diplomat. Then, suddenly, he fell silent and stared at me. I must have seemed puny to him, I thought, 'cause I sure *felt* puny, sitting across from him in this taxpayer-subsidized, top-floor executive dining room that I hadn't even known about until this morning.

Actually, I was struggling to translate in my head his seemingly artful[29] words, offered up in that classic State Department diplomatic doublespeak. I couldn't be mistaken, could I? Wasn't he urging me to stay in the Foreign Service and not to quit my career as a diplomat?

Talk about being confused. There was no enmity, no attack, no passion anywhere in his soul to get even. He just wanted me to stay.

"Harry," I said, "I've made so many enemies in this building." He knew who I was talking about. All those self-proclaimed experts who said they lived only for negotiating world peace, when all they really wanted was that next overseas assignment with its precious diplomatic immunity, rent-free living and tax-free booze the rest of America couldn't buy. I'd pissed them off. They knew it, I knew it, Harry knew it. Every last one of them had his knife out for me, and I'd been stuck in place because of it, with no chance of promotion.

"Pardon me for being the Brooklyn-mean-streets slob that everyone says I am," I went on, "there's not a snowball's chance in hell that I'm going to get anywhere anymore in the Foreign Service."

There! I said it.

"You're so wrong," he replied calmly. It would have taken only a feather to knock me off my chair as he continued: "I will make sure that you have two back-to-back assignments in Moscow after you go to Budapest. And don't worry about the promotion. It's going to happen no matter who wants to see you buried."

He stood up. I was speechless. Pushing back slowly from the table, I rose, not quite knowing what to do, what to say, then turned to look out of those floor-to-ceiling plate-glass windows overlooking the Mall, with the Lincoln Memorial out there to the right and C Street just below.

Harry had already countered my idea of quitting the State Department and maybe starting a consulting firm. "Consulting about what," he had retorted. "I don't know for sure," I had shot back. Now I was incredulous that he'd even think about committing to move heaven and earth so that it would all work out well for me—very well, indeed—as a senior U.S. diplomat. Nor was there any doubt in his mind or mine that he had the power to deliver on his commitment.

He must have known that he still hadn't made the sale to keep me in that jail. But I wasn't prepared for what came next.

As I was staring down at the street, his next comment hit me harder than my teammate back in Little League who, without meaning to do it, whacked me on the side of my head with his baseball bat.

"You know, Cliff, it's tough out there. Who's going to hire an unknown middle-level Foreign Service officer to do anything?"

As his toxic message burned my ears and my soul, a big truck slowly made its way around the parked cars on C Street seven stories below us. It had that huge, baby blue logo marking a truck leasing company that all of us here in the Baltimore-Washington metro area know for its sparklingly clean white vehicles:

"Brody Truck Rental."

"Go to hell, Harry. If *that* Brody can make it 'out there' by renting trucks, I ought to be able to do something worth something to someone 'out there,' too!"

Perhaps there are classier, visually more inspiring omens than these, but a truck just like the one on the right worked well for me then. And darned if they haven't been within sight many times since, just when I had tough choices to make...which have all turned out to be the right ones.

But did I really say that to Harry? Not by a long shot. I was talking to myself. As I grabbed his hand to quickly shake my good-bye, I looked him straight in the eye and shared only this: "Thanks, Harry. I've made up my mind. I'm out of here."

I never looked back.

What was wrong with Harry's commitment? Why was it suddenly so clear to me that his asking price was much too high for me to say "Yes" to the deal he was offering?

Your time is limited, so don't waste it living someone else's life.

Steve Jobs

To be nobody but yourself in a world which is doing its best, night and day, to make you everybody else means to fight the hardest battle which any human being can fight; and never stop fighting.

e.e. cummings, 1955

Change is inevitable—except from a vending machine.

Robert C. Gallagher

We all have big changes in our lives that are more or less a second chance.

Harrison Ford

The only man I know who behaves sensibly is my tailor; he takes my measurements anew each time he sees me. The rest go on with their old measurements and expect me to fit them.

George Bernard Shaw

We're about to uncover...

...the last two elements whose place in all commitments is critical.

As we cover this new ground, keep these two points from the preceding chapter in mind. First, for a commitment to work, you must acknowledge someone else's risk in trusting you. Second, you have to be flexible in dealing with changes arising during the lifetime of that commitment to maximize the odds that you'll keep that trust.

Now on to the last two elements of any commitment. Stated very simply, the first one is that you must be prepared to change your expectations for how most short-term and *all* long-term or lifetime commitments will work out.

To illustrate what this means, let's look at a short-term commitment. Let's say I commit to repairing your refrigerator and you commit to pay me $150 to do the work. The work took one day longer because the new part didn't arrive on time. Still, when I finish, the refrigerator actually works again, so you hand me a check, I deposit it, it clears the bank, and—voila!—the commitment has come to its desired end precisely because we both bent with the winds of change caused by the delay.

Now, let's think about a commitment that is meant to last a lifetime, but ends prematurely whether we want it to or not. Two people get married and then get divorced. AOL and Time/Warner merge and then break apart. We can turn our backs on the commitment altogether, as did Hitler to Stalin. Or we can go even farther by dropping it wholesale only to start it all over again, just like Tracy and Dexter did in *The Philadelphia Story*.

Ask yourself: did Tracy and Dexter really start their commitment all over again? Not by a long shot. It was clear at film's end that our two young Philadelphia patricians had quite different expectations tying the knot the second time around, and that they were agreeing to quite a different set of actions keep the second marriage commitment alive. Even though it sounded like the same thing when they agreed the second time around to "love, honor and cherish," those new expectations and actions translated into a Round 2 entirely different in substance than Round 1.

For long-term or lifetime commitments to work, they must survive a string of surprises, including many that could tear them to pieces. The preceding chapter hinted at a key ingredient for avoiding that result: showing enough flexibility along the way so that the other people in the deal keep on believing that working with you toward the agreed goal is still worth their while.

Often, the changes you have to make (or live with) are slight, even if they are vexing. Think of the repairman who calls to tell you he'll arrive tomorrow, not today, to fix your refrigerator, even though you waited all day for the fellow to show up. Other times, the changes are as profound as a caterpillar morphing into a beautiful butterfly: what comes out of that cocoon looks absolutely nothing like what went in, but aren't we ever thrilled with the night-into-day changes that have taken place!

If, then, it is a given that during the life of most every commitment there will be changes—sometimes even big ones—the companion truth is that once you make the first change, you are replacing the initial commitment with another one.

What I've just written in that last sentence isn't just clever wordsmithing. Instead, it is an important rule that applies to all commitments in which the basic goal remains the same but the people or actions change to fit new circumstance...and new expectations.

This can mean reworking the initial commitment so much so that, like the butterfly, what comes out looks nothing like what went in. Little matter, so long as what comes out is still centered on the original goal, or even a modified goal you all like. Outside events or interim results always bear down, sometimes hard, on what you thought would work but didn't. Being prepared to go with the flow and make the necessary adjustments is the ideal way to deal with this.

This brings us to the second of those last two elements of all commitments: being prepared to back out of a commitment even when the others in the deal want you to stay. A look at Bill and Hillary Clinton's marriage from 1998 to 2000 helps to define what this means.

Whatever other challenges the Clintons faced after disclosures surfaced about Monica Lewinsky, each Clinton was confronted with this question: given the radically altered post-disclosures reality that clearly threatened their marriage commitment, did either Clinton still want to be in this deal with the other?

Hillary Clinton had a companion challenge: did she want to be in a marriage commitment with a spouse who had so blatantly ignored her need to trust in his intent, his willingness, to make the marriage commitment work and to lessen her risk in taking him at his word?

It is not a stretch of logic to assume that in the first few weeks after publicity surfaced about Ms. Lewinsky, Hillary Clinton didn't like her husband very much. As if to make this point for her in his own October 9, 2009, late-night TV confession of sexual liaisons outside of marriage, David Letterman put matters this way: his own wife didn't like him very much right about then, he explicitly conceded, nor could anyone blame her for feeling the way she did.

But *like* and *trust* are two different animals. The United States never liked the Soviet Union but deeply trusted Moscow's commitment to launch hundreds of nuclear-armed intercontinental ballistic missiles towards U.S. cities if it sensed that any inbound American missiles were on their way to hit Soviet soil.

Nor did black Americans particularly "like" their Southern overseers during the heyday of Jim Crow laws or the Ku Klux Klan. There was no doubt, though, that they sure could trust the guys with the guns and the hoods and the hangman's nooses to enforce segregation.

The core issue confronting the Clintons or anyone when a commitment's underpinnings are threatened by a partner's ill-considered actions is whether the wronged partner still believes that it is worth his or her while to stay in the deal, and that enough trust can be rebuilt to keep the commitment going.

That phrase, "worth his or her while," refers not to whether someone likes the other person. Rather, it refers to whether the wronged partner—I repeat: the wronged partner—not only sees enough reason to trust the other partner but also believes that there is value to be received in return for giving the perpetrator what he or she wants *in the future.*

Good Lord! Does this then mean, for example, that Hillary Clinton had to agree to keep on giving things *to* Bill Clinton that *he* wanted, or that she would have work hard to keep the trust of the very partner who caused her grief in the first place? Am I really saying here that the aggrieved spouse who comes out on the short end of the stick in the deal now has to continue to be a "gift that keeps on giving" to the perpetrator?

Like it or not, the answer is "Yes!" For Hillary Clinton or anyone in similar circumstances to stay in the deal, she had to be willing in the future to give as much value to her husband as she wanted in return.

Keep in mind: regardless of what happened yesterday, staying in the deal—any deal—binds the partners to exchange matched values today and tomorrow. The nature of tomorrow's value might be different than yesterday's, even radically so—perhaps an ice-cold frappuccino instead of an extra hot latte. As we've said before, without that matched exchange of values, there is no commitment. And without the companion trust that goes along with the matched exchange, there is no commitment either.

Other women finding themselves in the same predicament as Hillary Clinton have made radically different choices. In 2009, Jenny Sanford, wife of then-South Carolina Governor Mark Sanford, surely did.

The in-your-face challenge she faced came on the heels of husband Mark's stark public admission in June of that year that, rather than hiking the Appalachian Trail when he dropped from sight over several days, he had been Absent Without Leave both from the state capital and his marriage while visiting his lover and "soul mate" in Argentina.

Jenny Sanford had to answer the same question as Hillary Clinton: will I still get as much value from this guy in the future as I myself have to give if I stay in this deal?

In her memoir[30] released a month before her petition for divorce was granted on February 10, 2010, Mrs. Sanford disclosed that, before her wedding, she was going into the marriage knowing that husband-to-be Mark was not sure he could stay monogamous. How? He had said so to her—explicitly—while they were engaged, and she had countered that she wanted him to stay faithful. As she herself later put it in her biography, Mrs. Sanford had thus taken a "leap of faith" that things would work out more to her satisfaction than his.

Think about it. Isn't "leap of faith" a great definition for trust? The leap doesn't even have to be blind: in Jenny Sanford's case, her leap was hardly blind at all. Not only did she know of the special risk she was taking when first entering into the marriage deal, her then-husband-to-be knew that her expectations ran counter to what he thought he might do.

Later in their marriage, when it became painfully clear to them both that he would not meet her expectations of monogamy, whether she liked him or loved him anymore[31] was of little consequence. She had lost all confidence that husband Mark could be trusted in the future to exchange anywhere near the same value—the monogamy that she wanted—even if she agreed to stay in the marriage as Mark proposed after returning home from Argentina.

What option did she choose instead? To end the commitment, no matter what husband Mark wanted.

Being prepared to end the commitment, even though others don't want you to do it, is that second of the last two commitment ingredients now under our microscope.

Unlike your being prepared to change the nature of the commitment when circumstances suggest doing so, this ingredient requires major courage: letting go of your own hopes and dreams. It is the very high price you'll always pay for making a tough decision others might strenuously oppose, namely abandoning a long-term or lifetime commitment once and for all.

Rolling with the punches as "change" hits you square on the jaw. Being prepared to end a commitment as the way to increase the odds of its succeeding.

Don't those two ideas sound self-contradictory? Which comes first? What comes next? What's the right order for mixing these two, and in fact, all nine ingredients into a commitment that actually works?

And what is the glue holding all the pieces together?

COMMITMENTS

13. What Glue Holds All The Commitment Ingredients Together?

Back to reality.

Suddenly the air horns are sounding. The trucks in front of me have started to move, the drivers behind me are screaming for me to get the hell out of their way, and there is no room to turn around or even to move to the side.

There is no way but forward.

******

I hadn't been so fearful, so stuck in place since my own terror 38 years earlier, during the 1968 Tet Offensive in Vietnam, when real people from North Vietnam were shooting real bullets at us while my guys and I were pinned down in place.

Now, the same fear was gripping me—but in a car stuck in traffic? Me, a battle-hardened veteran of the worst-of-the-worst bumper-to-bumper bottlenecks that the Long Island Expressway ever offered? What was wrong with this picture?

Here's what. After all my hard work to squeeze out every last possible surprise on this once-in-a-lifetime 10,000 mile road trip from

Washington DC to the Arctic Ocean , I was now stopped dead in my tracks just north of Fairbanks, frozen in place by something so unexpected.

I had 198 more miles yet to go before nightfall, due north into the Arctic just to reach halfway point Coldfoot, Alaska on this last 400 mile stretch. And suddenly: no more road! Instead, just softball-sized rocks being crushed crudely into place by a monster roller machine. The crusher was at the front of a flesh-and-metal parade of giant trucks in front of me and behind, all in single file, any and every one of their tires taller than my car.

And we were all waiting, like prisoners in a chain gang, until the road graders behind the crusher moved to the side and offered us passage onto the Dalton Highway.

This, a highway? A rutted dirt road was the Daytona Speedway compared to what lay before us.

Turn around! No, go forward! I can't get across all this in a car! I can! I must! No, don't go any farther, you fool! Yes you must, 'cause you've driven 6,000 miles just to get to the starting gate and can't afford to be stopped by this. Yes you can! Turn around! No, go forward. No! Yes! Yes! No!

Whatever I'm gonna' do, I better do it fast! Those truckers in their giant 34-wheelers[32] are staring at me from their cabs in disbelief, waiting for me to move or at least to get the hell out of their way.

I had been so intent on driving my well-worn 7-year-old BMW from Washington to Alaska's Prudhoe Bay on the Arctic Ocean, 200 miles above the Arctic Circle. It was a life's dream trip, cemented in my mind ever since 1949. I was 8 years old then, and someone on the radio was talking about the old World War II Alcan Highway being opened to public use. Eight years before I even got my learner's permit, I decided then and there: I was going to drive the Alcan Highway from one end to the other.

Now, staring at this rocky debris passing for a road, I am just plain frozen in place.

"What the hell are you doing, driving that car here?" shouts one trucker. "On this road?" I can hear him thinking as he stares at the Washington, D.C. license tag on the BMW's rear bumper: just how much out of their minds *are* those people in Washington?

Good question. On paper, it is hard to get lost driving in Alaska. Or in Canada's Northwest and Yukon Territories, for that matter, because there aren't more than a handful of main roads going anywhere.

Alaska itself has very few numbered highways, in fact, only thirteen. There's Highway 1, Highway 2, right up to Highway 12. For reasons unknown, what would have been Highway 13 is actually Highway 98.

All thirteen have way cool names, though, like the Dalton Highway, Glenn Highway, and Tok Cutoff (all Route 1!), Denali Highway (Route 7), and, best of all, the Klondike Highway (Route 98) from Skagway to the Yukon. Some of the unnumbered roads are equally amazing: try the Top of the World Highway that continues east from Chicken, Alaska to the western bank of the Yukon River at Dawson, in the Yukon. Extraordinary!

With only thirteen numbered through roads to choose from, you'd think it would be easy to get to where you want to go, right?

On just about every mile of those roads, guiding you every step of the way, there are these little orange flags. Such little things they are, but oh how they portend great surprises in store, and not happy ones, either.

Who puts all these life-saving semaphores alongside the road, the ones I learned so quickly to respect? What were the roots of the peculiar craft that drove—drives—such a small group of people to plant those little stakes in the ground? Why were these people making such a strong, lasting commitment to us, the hundreds of thousands of people they would never meet who travel these roads?

I found out soon enough.

In far northwest Canada and Alaska, the constant cycle of freezing and thawing twists once-flat surfaces of asphalt or gravel into roller-coasters of frost-heave ridgelines, whole mini-mountain ranges of sudden hills and deep valleys.

Every one of these frost heaves taunts you: "Come at me faster than a walker's pace, and I'll swallow you and your car! Or truck!"

Who were the first people, unknowing of whomever might come along afterwards, to give their gift of time and thought by planting the first roadside orange markers that called out: "Slow down, for your sake and God's alike!"

What do we give you in exchange that caused you to care about us? What did we and you exchange of equal value? How is our commitment to you, and yours to us, centered today, and how will it be centered tomorrow?

We'll never know who put them there. But aren't we glad they did!

Back to reality.

Suddenly the air horns are sounding. The trucks in front of me have started to move, the drivers behind me are screaming for me to get the hell out of their way, and there is no room to turn around or even to move to the side.

There is no way but forward.

Ever so slowly, me in my car, the trucks, all of us, hobbled along the rocky path until it became gravel, then broken pavement, then a brand new section of silky smooth blacktop.

And together we watched. We watched intently for those little orange flags stuck in the ground by hands unknown to make sure we slowed down enough to reach our goal.

What an Alaska Highway frost heave looks like in summer. If you're traveling more than about 20 miles an hour over something like this, you're on your way to the repair shop...and a hefty bill.

I still don't know who had helped us survive these roads. Nor do I really know why they continue to do it today. I know only to be ever grateful for their commitment to us.

The way a team plays as a whole determines its success. You may have the greatest bunch of individual stars in the world, but if they don't play together, the club won't be worth a dime.

Babe Ruth

I have found no greater satisfaction than achieving success through honest dealing and strict adherence to the view that, for you to gain, those you deal with should gain as well.

Alan Greenspan

The man who will use his skill and constructive imagination to see how much he can give for a dollar, instead of how little he can give for a dollar, is bound to succeed.

Henry Ford

If there are so many moving parts...

...to commitments, what glue holds them together?

Surprise! The glue is what we *want*, not what we *need*.

How else would I have gotten that refrigerator repaired? Maybe I wanted to spend that $150 somewhere else, or even to save it. But I needed to exchange it with the repair person *to receive back the value I really wanted:* his personal involvement, his expertise, his time and his tools to make the refrigerator work again. That, as it turns out, was the result I apparently wanted more than the feel of that money in my pocket, even though I didn't have to make that commitment at all and instead could have elected to go on without a working fridge.

And then there is that tale of the two dictators at the dawn of World War II. Both ended up wanting to do something they arguably didn't want to do at all—at first. But Hitler needed Nazi Germany's access to all those raw materials overflowing in the Soviet Union. So he wanted that nonaggression pact with Moscow big time, even though he loathed Stalin. For his part, Stalin needed to prevent Germany from using its own military machine to thwart Soviet land grabs in Central Europe. So he very much wanted to do a deal with Hitler, even if he detested the fact that he had to. All this said, they surely didn't have to do the deal; no one was pointing a gun to either's head.

The Clintons showed themselves willing to endure tremendous pain in overcoming enormous personal challenges arising from the president's errant actions. It could hardly be said that they wanted these challenges or were thrilled to do the work to surmount them. They surely didn't want to face all the public scrutiny, political and legal troubles (not to forget: the president was impeached!), and all the sleepless nights, either.

Why did the Clintons end up wanting to commit to something (continuing the marriage) by addressing those post-Lewinsky challenges they surely hadn't wanted in the first place? Because of what they really wanted more, which was to keep their family together. You and I do the same thing all the time. With our eyes wide open, we choose to do something we would prefer not doing because it will get us something else we want even more.

Economists call what we give up in this process the "opportunity cost" we pay. Loosely defined, that cost is any opportunity we give up by paying time, money or anything else for something we want more than the time or money we are giving up.

The opportunity cost I pay to get the refrigerator fixed is not the repairman's $150 fee, but instead the opportunity to use that $150 to buy something else. The opportunity cost to Stalin in his deal with Hitler was a "lasting" peace with Germany that cost him dearly when the Nazis invaded the Soviet Union soon after.[33]

One of the many opportunity costs Hillary Clinton paid was the time and energy, assets she otherwise might have spent on more pleasurable things, that she instead committed to rebuild equanimity and equilibrium within her family. We can only assume that this was something she dearly wanted but arguably didn't need in order to survive personal tragedy and live a rewarding life. Jenny Sanford's decision confirms how that might have unfolded.

Our desires—our *wants* —are what hold commitments together. We will give up a lot—paying a high opportunity cost—in the process. Why? Because we know that we can get what we want only by paying other people to help us get there, and using the structure of a commitment to do it.

Why do we commit to paying taxes to employ all those government workers, even though we don't like paying them? Because we need them in the deal to get what we really want. Why else would anyone be willing to pick up our garbage, fly those fighter jets into battle, or plant bright neon orange flags marking those otherwise invisible car-swallowing frost heaves in the road? How would we get any of the results we wanted if we didn't pay them?

Be careful if you're now thinking: "I do lots of things by myself without paying anyone anything!"

In your dreams you do! You cannot name one thing you supposedly do by yourself that does not actually involve someone, somewhere, doing something because of a payment you make to them, whether you're conscious of it or not.

Let's say you decide to write a book by yourself. Have you made a commitment only to yourself? If you decide to lose 10 pounds, can you do it all on your own? Fat chance! How on earth are you going to get those things done without paying someone else for something critical to your success? What about the computer you use? The electricity it uses? The food you buy to make the diet work? What you learned from someone else after buying and reading her diet book?

Perhaps you think all this talk about computers and electricity is too subtle. Would you really say that if the electricity went out? Think about it. Almost everyone's first reaction when the lights suddenly go out is: "What are they going to do about it?" (Hint: the key word in that question is "they"!) Later, when the power still hasn't come back on, you're thinking: "What is taking them so long?" (You get to guess what the key word is in *that* question!)

C'mon, people! When the lights go out, you don't think about the electricity that you thought you bought. You think about the people you have paid to keep the lights on.

In the wake of a tornado crushing the life out of our hometown, our wanting to help others is nice. Yet even this involves payment— which is really an exchange of equal values. Whether we're conscious of it or not, we help family, friends, neighbors and strangers in the aftermath of tragedies out of our own deep passion to get things back to the "normal" we dearly want and the emotional equilibrium we crave. So we end up not only wanting to help others pick up the pieces of their lives, but also lending our manual labor and contributed dollars to put the pieces of our own lives back together.

Why else, for example, would we work with someone from down the street, whom we may not even know, to clear the street of debris after a big thunderstorm? Why else, when we don't really know her at all, would we shovel the snow off the walkway to a neighbor's house?

No matter how we slice this "why-we-make-commitments" pie, the filling stays the same. We *want* to make commitments, even when we don't always like the price we are paying, because we need to pay other people to get what *we* really want.

There is more. We willingly enter into commitments to pay these others because we just plain don't like being alone. If I go out to a restaurant for a nice meal, I'll almost always want the company of someone else. Maybe it's my sweetheart. Maybe a friend. Maybe the new faces I'll see, and the new people I'll meet.

Whatever the case, I'll always commit to a trade. Perhaps it will be picking up the tab, offering up nice dinner conversation, or driving us there. Whatever it is, I am exchanging something of value with someone because even if I don't need it at all, I want another person in the room with me.

It works this way even in my sweetheart's book club. She cherishes each moment they meet, because it is so interesting for her to hear their thoughts about what she has just read.

Sure, she gets a lot out of reading the book herself. What is especially valuable to her, however, is discovering what her friends got out of the book, and the wine and snacks are always good. Better yet, the price she agrees to pay in exchange for the value they give her—their company—is so low: her "cost" is simply showing up at the meeting. She doesn't even have to say anything or read the book (though she always does both!) to get what she really wants out of the deal: plain good company.

Is it really that simple, that we make commitments because there is no other way to get what we want, regardless of whether we really need it?

And, can we really conclude that if those wants of ours are the reason why we make commitments, our wants are also the glue that holds all commitments together?

Actually, yes. In fact, this just about says it all regarding the tie that binds together all the moving parts of a commitment.

Almost all, that is.

COMMITMENTS

14. Commitments Are Too Complicated! Can't We "Uncomplicate" Them?

Everyone expected "charming," so charming is what they were going to get.

Wasn't it only three days after Hurricane Sandy had wreaked havoc on New York City and Long Island? Hadn't my son, his fiancée, and her family performed miracle after miracle in those 72 hours just after Sandy literally washed away the swish yacht club chosen for this magic day? Along with the lives and livelihoods of so many others?

Hadn't they pulled off the impossible by locating and nailing down this new venue for the ceremony and reception—and at one of New York City's most prized locations no less?

Hadn't everyone on the guest list moved heaven and earth to get here in this post-Sandy moment of no planes, no trains, and lines at the gas station that stretched for blocks?

Was I going to be the Grinch who stole *this* Christmas? Not hardly.

******

Why wasn't it easy? Just a few steps, arm in arm, she and I both dressed in elegant wedding day black. She was smiling too eagerly, I thought, but not looking half bad as she tucked her elbow close to my side to keep us together as the bridegroom's parents. We dance-stepped to the rhythm sweeping us into a large faux-baroque gold-gilded reception room overlooking all of New York City.

No one had told me that at this ceremony, I would actually have to say more than two words to my ex-wife, no less escort her, the two of us alone in the spotlight as if everything were just peachy-keen between us. I had come to be so comfortable with the vast distance between us that she and I had built. We had been civil in every respect, but without any warmth or charity in thought or deed. I had vowed never to be seen side by side with her again ever since a chance meeting on a Georgetown street two years after our divorce, when we shared a walk together in our old neighborhood.

Yet now, there we were together. I managed a smile while she strutted, much as if she were at the head of a grand military parade of victor over vanquished. No one seemed to sense just how defeated I felt. Except me, of course. So many oohs and aahs from all corners! Didn't we look grand, they were all shouting. And cheering!

What was wrong with me? Why was my nose so out of joint? It was just a few steps, a smile, a feigned kiss on the cheek. Oh the pain! Call it a self-inflicted wound if you want, and I'll take the rap. I just wanted that day to be much easier. If I had known all along that it would not be entirely pain-free, I at least felt I would have had a say in being near the people I liked but not near someone I had come almost to despise.

It was my son's wedding, right? Everyone was expecting "charming," so charming is what they were going to get.

Wasn't it only three days after Hurricane Sandy had wreaked havoc on New York City and Long Island?

Hadn't my son, his fiancée, and her family performed miracle after miracle in those 72 hours just after Sandy literally washed away the swish yacht club chosen for this magic day? Along with the lives and livelihoods of so many others?

On Long Island's South Shore, the day of the wedding, a sight to see...

...and the wedding site we saw, looking high over New York City at the posh Terrace on the Park in Flushing Meadows, as if Sandy had never happened.

Hadn't they pulled off the impossible by locating and nailing down this new venue for the ceremony and reception—and at one of New York City's most prized locations no less?

Hadn't everyone on the guest list moved heaven and earth to get here in this post-Sandy moment of no planes, no trains, and lines at the gas station that stretched for blocks?

Was I going to be the Grinch who stole *this* Christmas? Not hardly.

What was it I was so fond of telling others? Simple is not the same as easy. So simple to walk the few steps. So not easy! So difficult to put aside a seething anger that I will probably take to the grave. All this was reminding me of that other bit of advice I was so prone to give to others: Don't let anger eat you alive. If ever there was a day when I was living in a do-as-I-say-but-not-as-I-do world, it was this, my son's wedding day. Oh how my anger was eating me alive!

The crowd looked on. My son and his beautiful bride smiled, ear to ear. My "ex" pulled me onto the empty dance floor and I awkwardly led her in the slow waltz.

Oh how the pain of simple can be so hard to bear.

The truth is rarely pure and never simple.
Oscar Wilde

It's so simple to be wise. Just think of something stupid to say and say the opposite.
Sam Levenson

Guys are simple... women are not simple and they always assume that men must be just as complicated as they are, only way more mysterious. The whole point is guys are not thinking much. They are just what they appear to be. Tragically.
Dave Barry

I was a personality before I became a person—I am simple, complex, generous, selfish, unattractive, beautiful, lazy and driven.
Barbra Streisand

If the glue holding...

… commitments together is what we really want rather than just what we need, and if we add this notion to all the others uncovered till now…well…

Whew! At this point, you are probably thinking that commitments are nothing more than one big headache!

- We want things to be easy, not hard, and it sure looks like making commitments is much harder than we thought.

- No one likes pain, and commitments seem to be full of painfully hard work.

- No one likes admitting a mistake, yet commitments require us to acknowledge our mistakes when a commitment is not working or fails outright.

Or, maybe you are thinking that I am overcomplicating everything and that commitments aren't nearly as complicated as I'm making them out to be.

Maybe you're right.

Think cakes and pies. To bake a simple white cake, you need to mix together only a few basic ingredients: flour, sugar, butter, milk, eggs, a little baking powder, and vanilla extract.

Nominally, it is the same with "baking" a commitment. The main ingredients are goals, time, action, delivering the goods, trading equal values, placing your trust in others, and keeping someone else's trust in you.

Even better, the icing on this commitment "cake" has only two ingredients: recognizing the other person's risk in trusting you, and showing your own flexibility to make changes along the way.

Alas, while the ingredients in this recipe for the commitment cake may be easy enough to list and remember, it is the opposite of easy to mix them together in the right proportion and in the right sequence to get a well-formed, tasty culinary treat out of the oven—or better said in our case, the right results from a commitment.

Yet everyone increasingly seems to want "easy", especially today's younger generation according to popular print and online media commentaries. If today's Millennials' addiction to the Internet and social networking might have you thinking that the older among us are surely more willing to work harder for what we want, think again.

The human passion for "easy" is hardly unique to today's oft-criticized younger generation. Since the dawn of humankind, people have always wanted things to be easier. More importantly, every generation has expected that things would be easier for them than for the generations that preceded them.

In the sixteenth and seventeenth centuries, scholars wanted *and expected* the relative ease of finding knowledge in printed books at universities, rather than having to track down, as did their forebears, the single copy of a single written manuscript supposedly tucked away in a monastery perhaps a thousand miles away.[34] Those sixteenth and seventeenth century scholars had every right to consider books quite normal—and certainly much easier to use by comparison to those ancient manuscripts. You can bet, though, that their pre-Gutenberg[35] forebears certainly would have been complaining: "These young 'uns sure do have it easier than we did!"

Nor were there any rebellious colonists in late eighteenth century British North America who didn't know that, British oppression notwithstanding, they already had it much easier by comparison to the people who preceded them to the American continent 150 years earlier. Moreover, they considered their much easier lives to be quite normal but still not good enough. So they committed to a revolution that was very hard and costly to execute but, when all was said and done, one that did lift incredible burdens from everyone's shoulders. Freedom became much easier, even if still not totally easy...yet! At least we're on the right path...

People in the 1870's who boarded a train in St. Louis to travel to Oregon expected that their 10-day journey there and back would be much easier by comparison to forebears like Lewis and Clarke. Less than 70 years earlier, the Lewis and Clarke expedition needed almost *two years* to make the same cross-country round trip by foot, pack horses and a few small boats, the last of which they actually had to carry part of the way!

Just as we all expect life to be easier than it already is, we also want it to be pain-free.[36] A lot of people might consider *easy* and *pain-free* synonymous, or that pain-free is an example of what "easy" is.

However, I'm more comfortable with this idea: just as all human beings are born with a biological preference for sweet-tasting things rather than sour ones, we are actually born with a desire that life be easier than it actually is. In contrast, rather than us being born with an innate understanding of what emotional pain is, we go through an arduous process of learning what emotional pain is, with each of us eventually settling on our own personal definition.

This distinction, between an innate or genetically-anchored desire that things be easy—a desire that we're likely born with—and the emotional pain we learn while growing up, relates directly to commitments and whether they are too complicated. If emotional pain is an acquired taste, and I'm saying that it is, it then follows that we acquire a special edition of that pain when we discover one particular unhappy truth for the first time or rediscover it for the hundredth time: *People Rarely Live "Happily Ever After" When Commitments Fail.*

We may feel the searing pain of unrequited love for the first time, say, on the heels of breaking up with our first love. We aren't born with the knowledge of that pain; we learn it. Or we learn other painful truths of disappointment, ones that embed themselves so deeply within us that it takes years for them to surface. Too many children of an alcoholic or abusive parent know this awful learning process all too well. So do countless military veterans who live through the carnage of war, who then push that unique pain deep down inside, but who can't keep it bottled up forever. I certainly couldn't.

Statistically, there are a handful of people born with wiring so messed up that they genuinely cannot feel pain, are indifferent to it, or get to a point where they relish delivering it to others. Even the worst of sadistic serial killers, the ones who actually crave and savor the pain and death of people they don't know, have learned *how* to satisfy their perverse appetite: not a one of them was born with their destructive brand of "how-to" knowledge.

There is no exception to this rule of learning pain, either. Nor is there any escape from the awful truth that other people actually teach us what pain is. This includes hate, the most profound pain we can ever feel. As Lieutenant Cable so poignantly laments in *South Pacific:* [37]

You've got to be taught
To hate and fear
You've got to be taught
From year to year
It's got to be drummed
in your dear little ear
You've got to be carefully taught.

You've got to be taught
To be afraid
Of people whose eyes
are oddly made
And people whose skin
Is a different shade
You've got to be carefully taught.

You've got to be taught
Before it's too late
Before you are 6 or 7 or 8
To hate all the people
your relatives hate
You've got to be carefully taught.
You've got to be carefully taught!

If we learn pain including the pain of hate and hatred, and if commitments when they fail indeed carry the potential for delivering severe pain (including hatred), we will never know exactly what pain might emerge from a failed commitment until after the failure actually takes place.

Some pain can be estimated when, in negotiating the actions required in a commitment, the people making the deal are realistic with one another (and themselves) as to what might go wrong and what contingency planning might be necessary. In effect, they are building in some of that flexibility we talked about in earlier chapters.

Pain is understandably unforeseen, however, when no one could have realistically predicted what happened. None of the victims of the September 11, 2001 attack on the World Trade Center could have reasonably predicted what was about to unfold that day when they or their loved ones left for work that morning, most simply following through on something they had earlier committed to do.

There is more. Along with the emotional pain we learn to define and understand for ourselves, we also learn something else early on: that we don't like being known for making a mistake. We certainly don't like admitting to mistakes, especially when our mistake has caused pain to others, not just ourselves.

Earlier in this book, I noted that when a commitment is suddenly not working, the only way we can keep it on the rails is by acknowledging what is going wrong, why, and how we have to change in response to changed circumstances.

There is a companion truth: *We ourselves* are the main reason most commitments go wrong. Except for those few cases where problems have been caused solely by forces beyond anyone's control, we ourselves—and especially what we've done—are almost always a major part of the snags we now want to untangle.

What part in this are we really playing? Well, somewhere along the way, you may have heard that the definition of insanity is doing the same thing over and over and expecting the results to be different.[38]

164

Applying this idea to commitments, don't be fooled into thinking that the only solution is changing what you do for tomorrow's commitment to work out better than yesterday's. For, the real answer is that you probably have to do the same things you did before *but in a different order,* and usually much earlier than the last time around. You must also figure out what you were doing right but simply didn't do enough of.

How to do all that during a commitment, before it fails? Get everyone to agree at the very beginning to a couple of ground rules.

One, that no one will ever use labels like bad, dumb or wrong to describe anyone else's actions, no matter how well or poorly the commitment works out.

Two, that no one will be nailed for raising a problem sooner rather than later.

And three, that no one will be told that "You have to change!"

Following these three ground rules are the way to uncomplicate commitments.

Is doing these three things simple and easy? Well, they are surely simple to talk about doing, but if anything they are the exact opposite of being "easy" to do.

Agreeing to hold back on name-calling and then asking other people to recognize a problem you see but they don't—or won't—is hard. Doing it early enough to allow enough time and thought for solving the problem is even harder, especially when you find yourself the only one with the guts to insist that everyone else face the music, not just you.

No matter how hard it is, it is well worth the effort, since tackling a problem that everyone would rather ignore is a fundamental feature of every commitment that works. Why? Because it makes it much, much easier for everyone to accept only a share of the responsibility— not all of it—when commitments are not working out as expected, and to work together to find alternatives to keep the commitment on the rails.

If no-name-calling and earlier intervention are key to commitments that work, is there anything else just as critical?

Yes. Making sure the pill of owning a mistake goes down without killing the patient. How? By agreeing that your (or anyone's) owning up to a mistake does not mean that the person has to "change". Rather, she or he simply has to change *when* "who" should be doing "what" to get to where everyone wants to be.

These simple ground rules, no name calling, raising problems sooner rather than later, and changing the order of people's actions rather than trying to change people themselves, will make it much easier to make and keep commitments, pinpoint what's not working well and why, and figure out a better way to get to where you all want to go.

So, here we are at last, at that question of questions: can doing all this stuff guarantee that the commitments you make will actually succeed?

15. When It Looks Like the Commitment Is Really Failing!

As we listened to her making the same profane point over and over again, we were staggered less by the profanities she was screaming than by how often she repeated them. Literally word for word. Lord, how deep did this infection reach into her soul?

Then, as suddenly as it began, there was silence. Had she worn herself out? More silence. Dear T in Florida. Me in Washington. DJ in New Jersey. No one's speaking. Normally Mr. Loquacious, I'm at a total loss for what to say next.

******

Neither T nor I knew what was about to hit us. DJ's outburst came out of the blue, dark, venal, laden with loathing of all that I was and had ever been. I was hearing my mother all over again, from 50 or 60 years ago.

Oh how My Dear Mom could lose it in her so-well-practiced ways that only did more to underscore her own self-hatred than anything she saw as less than the best in me.

Maybe like My Dear Mom, DJ also had no other way to get her point across. All she could do at that moment was to repeat the same epithets again and again, over a now red-hot phone line. Poisonous fetid water by the gallons overflowed the dam of her paper-thin veneer of sophistication.

Fury. No matter what its source, nature or humankind, its force is so destructive.

As we listened to her making the same profane point over and over again, we were staggered less by the profanities she was screaming than by how often she repeated them. Literally word for word. Lord, how deep did this infection reach into her soul?

Then, as suddenly as it began, there was silence. Had she worn herself out? More silence. Dear T in Florida. Me in Washington. DJ in New Jersey. No one's speaking. Normally Mr. Loquacious, I'm at a total loss for what to say next.

Finally T's hesitant, breaking, tearful voice filters through: "I ... I think ... Let's calm down. This is going too far."

DJ's words had not been the lines of some new script she had just pulled out of an envelope for a first review. Her terse little word picture of how utterly worthless I was to all humanity had spilled over from long ago.

Then, in a flash, the last pieces of an unfinished puzzle I had been ignoring over the decades began to fall into place: T and I had undermined DJ's penchant for using her wealth to get the rest of the world to do what she wanted. So used to having her own way, she had never learned how to reap the benefit of building a consensus. She had never enjoyed the luxury of leading people with ideas instead of dollars.

She just didn't know how.

It also seemed just then that all the empathy in the world couldn't change where matters now suddenly stood: hadn't irreparable damage been done? It was to be easily papered over in the months that followed, but a great frozen wasteland between the two of us remained.

Of course, even then I knew that if push came to shove, I would lay down my life for DJ without a second's hesitation. But for the longest time, I wasn't too keen on having dinner with her.

Or even lunch.[39]

When I was about nine, my siblings and I fell out of our moving van at an intersection. My dad didn't notice for about five blocks. It was back before seat belts. It was also back before parents used any sort of common sense whatsoever. It was a time when you didn't raise your children. You just fed them and they got bigger.

Dina Kucera, Everything I Never Wanted to Be

She wanted to ask him why they were all strangers who shared the same last name.

Chimamanda Ngozi Adichie, Half of a Yellow Sun

Talent wins games, but teamwork and intelligence wins championships.

Michael Jordan

The real test is not whether you avoid ... failure, because you won't. It's whether you let it harden or shame you into inaction, or whether you learn from it; whether you choose to persevere.

Barack Obama

Three simple rules...

...—no name calling, raising problems sooner rather than later, and focusing on how actions rather people should change—will make even the most complicated commitments easier. However, there is no guarantee that doing these things along with everything else outlined up to now, your commitments are sure to succeed.

There is some good news, though. You can take smarter, better steps to detect when a commitment may be failing. And, you can do it in enough time to keep the commitment on the rails, or at least to end it in ways that will make it easier for you to make the next one.

The first of these smarter, better steps is knowing the difference between a commitment that is actually failing and one that has merely run into problems.

Whether short-term or long-term, all commitments can become problematic. The replacement parts don't arrive on time and you have to wait out the delay before the refrigerator is repaired. The financial advisor to whom you entrusted your retirement account calls with the bad news that one of your stocks went way south. Your flight is cancelled and your three-day weekend in the Bahamas is evaporating fast. The cable TV repair guy doesn't show up.

In each of those examples, you have a Hobson's Choice: either bend with the problem winds that are blowing or end the commitment. There is no third choice.

You can still get the refrigerator repaired, but you'll have to wait until tomorrow. You can reinvest what's left of your money in something else. You can find another flight to Nassau. You can set up another appointment with the cable company.

When the goal is tangible, it is fairly simple to decide whether a commitment is simply in need of an adjustment rather than in deep, deep trouble. You can see and touch the refrigerator, the monthly account statement from your broker, the airplane ticket in your hand, or the cable box that has stopped working.

The opportunity cost is equally simple to calculate. And easy, too! We measure any delay in refrigerator repairs by days and maybe the dollars for replacing any food that spoils. That's easy, not just simple. Dollars also make it easy to measure your investment losses. If you don't get another flight to Nassau soon, you will lose your deposit on the hotel room—dollars again. As for the cable guy, well, there goes another half-vacation day you'll have to pay so you can be there for the next try.

In each case, you're measuring the actual cost *very* easily, that is, in dollars or hours, even if you don't like the fact that you have to spend that extra time or money in ways you didn't expect.

Is it just as simple and easy when the commitment is centered on something intangible, such as to love, honor and cherish till death do us part?

Actually, it is just as simple to decide that an intangible commitment is in trouble, so long as you also remember something else, too: that there is a vast difference between "simple" and "easy." That is, while it is just as simple to detect when a commitment centered on intangibles is in trouble, it isn't anywhere near so easy to decide what to do next.

There are many reasons why. First, it is much harder to measure both the actual cost and the opportunity cost of working towards an intangible goal that suddenly seems less likely to be fulfilled. (Remember that the opportunity cost is the other opportunities you have given up to get what you want in *this* deal.)

How do I calculate what am I paying—or losing—when I believe someone who's supposed to be loving, honoring and cherishing me simply isn't? Is the opportunity cost the lost chance to marry someone else I knew and loved 20 years ago?

What about my child who, after I've helped him for an hour, promises to finish his homework, does exactly that, and then cannot remember the formula for calculating a circle's diameter that he just studied? What about a U.S. president who says he'll do everything possible to improve education and then doesn't? There is no escaping it: calculating the opportunity cost to us is very, very hard when we run into problems trying to reach an intangible goal.

There is a second reason why it is harder to know when a commitment to something intangible is in trouble: *it is very difficult, sometimes even impossible, to measure the progress we're making towards an intangible goal.*

Think about it: when the goal is concrete, we easily and habitually use time, money and quantity to measure our progress: how close we are to saving for a down payment, how much time remains until a deadline, how much more tilling the garden soil needs before we can plant, or how many more bolts I must tighten before the Ikea bookshelf is assembled.

By contrast, it is hard to know how much you have done so far— and how much more you have to do—to love, honor and cherish someone. Sure, there are tangible things in that kind of commitment: flowers that I buy (or not) for my wife, the birthday I remember (or not), a "please" or a "thank you"—you get the idea. In each instance, though, the core commitment is what I said that I would do, usually over a long period of time, to make someone feel good and be happy.

There is one more reason why it is harder to detect when an intangible commitment is in trouble. Judging that we have successfully met our intangible goal is almost impossible because most intangible commitments never end.

Does celebrating our fortieth wedding anniversary mean that we have reached love-honor-and-cherish nirvana and that there is no more to be done? Has the Alcoholics Anonymous participant who refused a glass of wine at a party met his commitment in full?

If you're thinking that all of this is a matter of opinion, you're right! Beware! When it is all a matter of opinion, the major potential exists for incorrectly concluding that a tangible or intangible commitment is failing when all that may be required is just getting past a bump in the road.

Aha! We have just uncovered the word that counts for a whole lot: opinion! What do we do about reconciling different opinions about how well we're doing—or not—in meeting a commitment to do something, especially one with a wholly intangible goal?

Here's what. At the very outset of any commitment, but especially when the goal is intangible, everyone in the deal must be up front and explicit in accepting that down the road, each person's opinion will be his or her primary driver in judging whether others are doing what they've promised to do.

All of you then have to agree on a process for consensus building when your opinions conflict—which from time to time they surely will. This consensus-building process requires a willingness on everyone's part to borrow something from Person A's opinion, something from person B's, and so on, to build a consensus about how to get past any problem presenting itself along the way. Remember: no one's opinion will prevail all the time, and your consensus may turn out to be to abandon the commitment altogether.

Here's a real-life example:

When our children were young, four and seven years old respectively, the four of us made an actual commitment to consensus building as the best way for trying to resolve conflicts between or among us.

The rule was simple: at any point any parent or child could call a family meeting, at which time we all had to gather around the kitchen table within five minutes and give the gavel to the person calling the meeting.

There were only two caveats. First, everyone had to be at home; if not, the meeting was set for when the missing person showed up. Second, the meeting could not prevent anyone from honoring a prior commitment to be somewhere else at the appointed time.

Our four-year-old was immediately delighted with her power to call everyone to the table, and at first there were two or three meetings a day. Soon after, however, she tired of the process, realizing the major hit on her own time these sessions were costing her—the high opportunity cost to her of wielding so much power.

While we continued to honor every one of her family meeting calls, she quickly learned how to preserve her authority (and time) only for those issues that really counted a lot to her, ones that she felt were truly worth her time. It was a great lesson in developing skills at prioritizing, and we all honed them, not just her. And, while our summits didn't work every single time, the majority did—and well.

Whatever process you choose for achieving it, consensus building is the only opportunity for everyone in any commitment to decide whether:

a. what you've been doing all along is still fine, or

b. what you've been doing all along is not so fine and you need to change what you're doing to get to the original goal, or

c. you should end the commitment once and for all.

Before embarking on an explicitly-agreed commitment involving two or more people, making the effort to agree on a *process* for reaching this kind consensus is one of those smarter, better steps to which you should devote as much time, thought, and effort as is humanly possible.

Then, and like nothing else during the life of any commitment, using this consensus building process will arm every one of you with a much better understanding of:

– what is going well or not,

– what and how things could go or have gone better,

– why you even thought about ending the deal but decided not to,

– why you did end it (if that happens) before reaching your goal, and

– valuable lessons learned when the time comes for making the next commitment.

It is time, now, to bite the bullet and state exactly when a commitment has failed.

A commitment fails when any one person involved in it says: "It's over!" Until that happens, at worst a commitment is failing.

Hopefully, everyone in the deal will wisely and sparingly wield this power to bring the curtain down on the show before the end of the play—and only after trying hard to reach consensus with every other commitment partner to reach the intended goal. Why? Because there is no going back once anyone in the deal says it is over.

A word to the wise here: it is easy to conjure up a scenario where, in the heat of the moment, someone screams out: "That's it! The commitment's over! I'm outta here!" Or words to that effect.

Train yourself never to use them or anything close to them when you are angry, unless you are absolutely sure you want to bring the commitment crashing down (Beware: being on solid ground in *anything* when you are angry is a neat trick very few of us can pull off). Those "I'm outta here!" words or anything akin to them are as corrosive to a commitment as the worst of cheating, lying, or stealing in a relationship...they will cut to the bone anyone else's confidence that the commitment has any chance of succeeding,

Giving a run at consensus building is always the much better, wiser option. It allows everyone the opportunity to figure out with much less emotion and much more careful thought whether and how to keep the deal going.

You may ask: does this consensus-building process ever require putting the blame at someone's feet for things that are going wrong?

What would you think if the answer were yes, but that it *always* meant placing blame at *your* feet?

COMMITMENTS

16. So The Commitment Failed After All! Who's To Blame?

Some might say I was too hasty to walk away from the venture. Others might say I was hard-hearted. Or pig-headed.

I knew that if our commitment to the venture's success was ever going to work, we'd both need to make some trade-offs from the nominal perfection she sought. Or that I sought.

Yet for me, now, it was obvious that the ultimate mistake had been mine, not hers. I had bet on a horse—a venture, not the person— that couldn't finish a tough race.

******

It wasn't necessary to read between the lines. Her anger spilled over with acid clarity. I wasn't paying enough attention to what she wanted or needed.

"I am unhappy with your refusal to address the heart of this issue, which is our communication." Now at last convinced that I would never be willing to face that problem head-on, she had concluded that we could not go on working together.

The speaker was my soon-to-be business partner, a creative if headstrong author and brilliant performing artist—in truth, a genius with few equals. However, her my-way-or-the-highway approach in managing her business affairs had been her biggest barrier to financial success until now. Making matters worse, she was all too often hung up on the style of how someone was telling her something rather than centering on the message's substance. And what a passion she had for sidestepping bad news!

Still, I couldn't believe she was pulling the plug. We had devoted months to close-hewn business planning and accounting, often working till the wee hours drafting one critical business document after another to support a major capital raise for her business. I had bet all my time and a good bit of money to bring her creative genius to market. And now it was all shot to hell.

Could this really be happening just because one or two business challenges that needed attention were out-of-bounds to her? Apparently so. It had made little difference how we might go about taking up these challenges. She kept insisting that we weren't going to discuss them. Period.

"But we have to!" I urged.

"Didn't you hear me?" she screamed. "Don't you see what's wrong with how we communicate?"

"No, actually," I replied. "There's nothing wrong with how we 'communicate.' Disagreeing about what we have to do next has nothing to do with understanding where you're coming from on this stuff, and you very well understand where I'm coming from. Let's not make this issue any different than it is. We disagree, that is that, and we've both got enough smarts to solve what's in the way of our getting new money. If we want the dough, that is. So what do you want to do?"

That answer came a few days later in her e-mail: "I am unhappy with your refusal to address the heart of this issue, which is our communication."

I stared at her words for a moment, and then it was suddenly clear. There was no more point in my giving this venture any more time, thought, money, or the value of my capital-raising network.

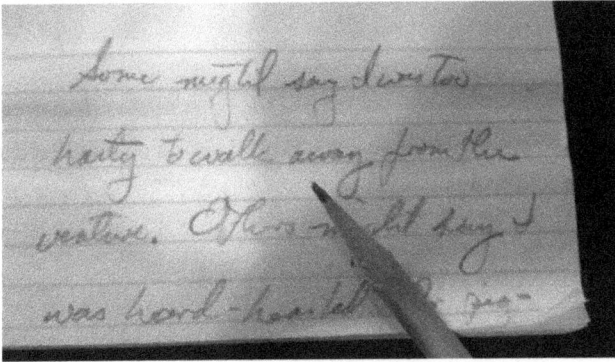

An author's note on a saga of failure with another author

Some might say I was too hasty to walk away from the venture. Others might say I was hard-hearted. Or pig-headed. I knew that if our commitment to the venture's success was ever going to work, we'd both need to make some trade-offs from the nominal perfection that she sought. Or that I sought.

Yet for me, now, it was obvious that the ultimate mistake had been mine, not hers. I had bet on a horse—a venture, not the person— that couldn't finish a tough race.

In the end, we had to move forward, rather than just move on. Which is what we did. Except that from then on, we moved forward on separate paths after I decided to end a commitment that for good reason I had once thought could be successful but about which, again for good reason, I had now changed my mind.

I alone am responsible and accountable for that decision. Not her.

You build on failure. You use it as a stepping stone. Close the door on the past. You don't try to forget the mistakes, but you don't dwell on it. You don't let it have any of your energy, or any of your time, or any of your space.

Johnny Cash

Mistakes are always forgivable, if one has the courage to admit them.

Bruce Lee

There are two ways of attaining an important end, force and perseverance; the silent power of the latter grows irresistible with time.

Sophie Swetchine

Anybody can become angry—that is easy, but to be angry with the right person and to the right degree and at the right time and for the right purpose, and in the right way—that is not within everybody's power and is not easy.

Aristotle

If there are smart ways...

...to tell the difference between commitments that are facing real problems and ones that actually are failing, and if there are effective ways to deal with the ones that are still alive but in trouble, the question then arises: who's to blame if a commitment does fail?

Like it or not, you're to blame when a commitment fails, in equal proportion to everyone else in the deal—no matter who you are, what the commitment was, when you made it, or what you did or did not do to make it happen.

To be clear, we're not talking about your being blamed for making the decision to end a commitment. The more important issue is this: who did or did not do everything needed to get the deal done as intended?

Here's a clue to what this means. Many decades ago when I was young, we used to say: "It takes two to tango." That pithy little catchphrase is normally meant to convey that it takes at least two people to get anything good done.

The mirror image of that catchphrase reads something like this: "It takes two to screw up." Living by this rule is the hardest part of making, changing, dropping or ending a commitment.

Yes, to make a commitment work, we have to be involved. We have to do something, not just sit there. And, try as we might, no matter how involved we are or how good our intentions may be to get the job done well, we're fated to make mistakes along the way.

Do we make these mistakes all by our lonesome selves?

In the previous chapter, I recommended that, when people first make a commitment, they should agree to a consensus-building process for solving problems that will arise along the way. If we know what that process includes, we will better understand how to deal with blame. Here it is:

- announcing sooner rather than later that something is troubling you about the way things are going.

- agreeing, then, to meet at an actual time and place to discuss what's bothering you, and scheduling that meeting at least one hour but preferably at least one day *after* you first voice your concern (unless the situation is truly dire or life-threatening and requires immediate action).

- staying on topic—what may be going wrong—once you sit down and start talking.

- leaving out any name-calling (you *must* stick to this rule).

- accepting responsibility (blame!) for your part in the problem and in the solution.

Don't think about a comeback like: "Well, Joe or Mary or Steven or John *is* the problem!" That response points the finger right back at you for not intervening earlier to help them do better than they did.

Keep in mind: People are people, not mistakes. We are all human, and we will make mistakes all the time! When you're trying to dissect a problem and come up with the solution, the process will be much easier and more effective if you assure your partners that you have an equal share in what went wrong, even if it is not immediately clear why, and that you will work with everyone else to find a solution.

When analyzing what went wrong, you may very well conclude that just one of you did something specific at a specific time that didn't work well, didn't work at all, or didn't sit well with the others. That is exactly what happened in the immediate aftermath of the Andrea Doria sinking off Nantucket in 1956. [40]

Not so fast. The unfolding aftermath of the Andrea Doria sinking amply confirmed why you can't simply point the finger at an "easy" culprit. Instead, you can and should work hard to figure out what you might have done to help that person avoid the mistake.

The sinking of the Italian ship Andrea Doria (first photo) when, late on July 25, 1956 off Nantucket, it turned left instead of right and was broadsided by the Swedish liner Stockholm (second photo). The rush to judgment: the crew on the Andrea Doria's bridge was to blame. But the accident investigation confirmed that the crews on both ships' bridges shared equal responsibility.

Maybe you'll decide there was nothing you could have done. Or something. Either way, it is worth the effort, because you will learn more about how to keep the current commitment going and how to avoid problems the next time around.

The beauty of the consensus-building process is that it has everyone in the deal figuring out what you all can do to help the team avoid a repetition of whatever hasn't worked well. This teamwork in consensus building is a major part of the magic of making commitments actually work.

Remarkably, this magic is also a foolproof test for who should be in the deal, especially when something goes astray. People who cannot own up to their share of the responsibility will always be too focused on fingering someone else rather than pulling their fair share of the weight. People who cannot ask themselves what they could have done better as part of the team are no more than "good-time Charlies," free-riders who won't do their share of the hard work needed for getting good things done.

It is best to find out who's a good-time-Charlie before sealing the commitment deal in the first place. How? Just ask at the very beginning whether everyone will commit to figure out what they could have done to help someone else avoid mistakes. You'll learn a lot!

Of course, while it is critically important always to take responsibility for your share of making a commitment work and also getting it back on the rails when it isn't, it is also possible to overdo these *mea culpas* and make matters worse. You are about to discover how.

17. After the Failure? It's Practice Without Perfection (Huh?)

The first lap goes OK. So does the second and third. I'm counting, counting…panting, panting…these boots are so heavy…God, please help me.

Lap four, then five. What's the time? How much do I have left? Lap six. My heart is pounding its way out of my chest. Nothing hurts anymore. Everything hurts now. I'm close to the end of lap seven now, but it seems all to be going too slowly, too slowly.

I look up: the three sergeants are watching me now, not the stopwatch. No smiles, just intense stares. What is going on? Then, like a bolt of lightning, the fourth NCO, the one I had never seen before, is running alongside me. "C'mon, Brody, c'mon. Only two laps left, you can do it!"

Oh My God! What does he mean? Two laps? I just did the seventh. There should only be one! Oh Lord! I miscounted. I'll *never* make it now!

******

I hated the Army. No, I didn't hate the Army at all, actually. I just hated being *in* the Army.

Perhaps it was the regimentation. Or maybe it was the seeming simple-mindedness that I saw (so arrogantly and incorrectly!) in all the drone-like people around me.

Top: Troops training at Fort Indiantown Gap, Pennsylvania, during World War II; Bottom: The same barracks today, where I trained in mid-summer 1963. The more things change...

Or perhaps it was the dispiriting, dehumanizing effect of sleeping 40 to a barracks with no walls or privacy. Or was it that horrible, scratchy recording of reveille screeching out over the loudspeakers at 5:15 every morning? Truth is, it was all these things and a whole lot more.

In short, I couldn't see any difference between Army basic training in that summer of 1963 and all I had read about Siberian labor camps. I especially hated the anonymity of the regimentation.

All my friends back home hadn't even bothered with ROTC. They didn't need the money like I did to get through college. Most of them were probably lying on some beach somewhere right now while I was stuck in a forgotten corner of Pennsylvania artfully known as Indiantown Gap. They were free as the wind, while I was just one of ten thousand recruits being taught how to obey orders, baking under a hot sun at a made-over World War II army infantry training base near Harrisburg.

Our only escape every sundown was to walk over to yet another run-down barracks that passed loosely for an enlisted men's club, where we could drown out the day's misery with some god-awful stuff they called near-beer.

What a waste of money, I thought while watching all the other guys downing bottle after bottle. What did they know that I didn't to find pleasure in that witch's brew? Wasn't I the smarter one for keeping my cash in my pocket! Well, that's what I thought, anyway.

The worst of the worst that summer was all that PT[41] in the morning, and the sword of Damocles that the drill sergeants had hung over my head: either I ran a mile in eight minutes or less, or I'd be doing basic training over again, right from the start, next summer.

Didn't they know that Jewish college kids from New York City didn't run miles? We just took the bus, the subway, or a cab everywhere! At least that was the way it used to be back in the early 1960s, before anyone knew how to spell *jogging*, before there were bike lanes on city streets, and *Nike* was still just the Greek goddess for victory.

Nor would I be running that Indiantown Gap mile in shorts and a T-shirt. Not hardly. It was eight laps in 90-degree muggy heat around a dusty eighth-mile track in full winter-weight combat gear, sporting a forty-two pound pack, a foxhole shovel banging against my thigh every step of the way, heavy, black leather combat boots weighing a ton each, a full canteen dangling from my web belt and, last but hardly the least, a genuine and very heavy M-1 rifle, a relic that had actually seen service during WW II and Korea.

Running the mile? How about wearing this gear and more,
plus combat boots, canvas army fatigues, and while you're at it,
why not stir in some humid 90+ degree weather? You get the idea...

Every other foul-mouthed grunt from my barracks had needed only one or two tries to do their mile in "less than eight." Some even did it in much less than eight minutes! Not me. I couldn't even finish my second attempt. Worse, in the days since, I was gripped with fear that I'd never pull it off and thus be doomed—three strikes and yer out!—to a worse-than-death hell of repeating all six weeks of basic training next year.

Finally, one bright morning, the moment of truth came. Me, my rifle, my backpack, and all the rest of my gear. There was no one else at the track, except for three grinning drill sergeants. One had made no secret of how he didn't think I would ever make it. Oddly, there was a fourth sergeant off by himself, just watching. I'd never seen him before. Who was he?

Off I go. I'm going to do it. I'm going to do it. I'm the little engine that could. No watch to pace myself, just those three goons standing there. The one with stopwatch in his hand wasn't even paying attention anymore. How am I doing? *How am I doing?*

I hate this place!

The first lap goes OK. So does the second and third. I'm counting, counting...panting, panting...these boots are so heavy...God, please help me.

Lap four, then five. What's the time? How much do I have left? Lap six. My heart is pounding its way out of my chest. Nothing hurts anymore. Everything hurts now. I'm close to the end of lap seven now, but it seems all to be going too slowly, too slowly.

I look up: the three sergeants are watching me now, not the stopwatch. No smiles, just intense stares. What is going on? Then, like a bolt of lightning, the fourth NCO, the one I had never seen before, is running alongside me. "C'mon, Brody, c'mon. Only two laps left, you can do it!"

Oh My God! What does he mean? Two laps? I just did the seventh. There should only be one! Oh Lord! I miscounted. I'll *never* make it now!

"Dammit, Brody. Pick it up. You gotta do two more!"

I have to do two more? I have to run faster, that's what I have to do! I can't come back here for another six weeks. I just can't! Run faster now, forget the pounding, forget the pain, forget the impossible burden of carrying all this stupid stuff on my back, forget everything! Damn them all!

I'm rounding the last turn for lap seven. How much time left to do the eighth? I don't know. Why work this hard for a lost cause? I pass the line to start the eighth lap. Is there enough time? For Christ sakes, tell me!

And then I hear it: "Stop! That's it!"

Out of time, and a whole lap to go? Son of a bitch! *SON OF A BITCH!*

All three of them are staring at me now. Then the one says: "Why didn't you do that the first time around?"

"Do what?"

"Six-and-a-half minutes, Brody. Never thought you could pull that off!"

I looked around to find that bastard who had frozen me with the fear of running the extra lap that wasn't.

He was gone.

The difference between perseverance and obstinacy is that one comes from a strong will, and the other from a strong won't.

Henry Ward Beecher

Consider the postage stamp: its usefulness consists in the ability to stick to one thing till it gets there.

Josh Billings

You learn you can do your best even when it's hard, even when you're tired and maybe hurting a little bit. It feels good to show some courage.

Joe Namath

Most people never run far enough on their first wind to find out they've got a second.

William James

When your dreams turn to dust, vacuum.

Author Unknown

So, we have just discovered...

...that if you want a commitment to work, you have to mix together these nine ingredients:

1. Goals.
2. Time.
3. Actions.
4. Delivering the goods.
5. Trust.
6. Trading equal values.
7. Keeping someone else's trust in the deal (and in you).
8. Accepting that no lifetime commitment will ever last a lifetime without changes.
9. Being prepared to end a commitment.

Once you've done all that, there is only one thing left: learning how to cope with the inevitable uncertainty built into any commitment, whether large or small, tangible or intangible.

Uncertainty. Whether it is refrigerator repairs or your marriage, you can never know that things will work out until they do. In fact, you may never know for sure, particularly for those intangible commitments like "until death do us part".

This uncertainty and the uneasiness that comes with it are not commitment ingredients and instead consequences of making commitments.

For example, we say that you have to earn and keep someone else's trust if you want that person to trust you the way you trust him or her. We've added in: you have to understand other people's risk in trusting you, as do the other people when it comes to understanding the risk you are taking by trusting them.

These elements are actual parts of an actual commitment structure, much like nuts and bolts are part of the bicycle you might assemble for your child's birthday present. The uncertainty of not knowing how easy or hard it will be for your child to learn to ride the bike is not a part of the bike itself, but rather a consequence of building the bike and how well you then teach someone else to ride it, steer it, and stop it.

The same goes for commitments. After the commitment is made, you must live day to day with the uncertainty that goes along with not ever quite knowing how the commitment will turn out—until it has reached one or another ending, that is.

Try these uncertainties: Will he show up? Will she love me tomorrow?[42] Will the president make sure there are no new taxes? Will Germany keep its promise not to invade? How many minutes, hours, days, weeks, months or years are we going to have to endure the uncertainty of not knowing for sure?

"As long as it takes!" is about the only answer there is.

Remember our discussion about Gabby Douglas? As did every one of her teammates, she had to practice, practice, practice. It was a given that there would be pain every step of the way, including the emotional pain of making mistake after mistake at the gym, with the coach reminding her, gently or not, that she was not only messing up but could never know in advance whether she'd make it to the Olympics, no less be a gold medal Olympic champion.

The sports clichés of "No pain, no gain!" and "practice makes perfect" apply as much to the uncertainty of commitments as they do to any athlete's training. As painful as it may be (and it is!) to practice making peace with the unknowns of how a commitment will unfold over time, each time you do gets you closer to perfection, making the uncertainty ever easier to endure.

Better still, you will learn how *not* to beat up on yourself when problems actually do surface, and to be ever more comfortable with this fact of life: problems are an inevitable consequence of future uncertainty, no matter how much we think we can avoid them.

Sure, when unwelcome issues surface or a commitment doesn't work out, you may be disappointed, even deeply so. But should you also be mixing a heavy dose of self-criticism into that disappointment? Most people do, whether consciously or not.

Given the real-life agony of carefully making, waiting out and keeping commitments, you can and should work hard to avoid self-criticism when a commitment seems to be in trouble, actually fails, or you end it before it fails.

How? By remembering your underlying successes in getting as far as you did. After all, you took a risk, you gave it a good run, and you can work every lesson learned either into fixing the commitment at hand or into the next one you make.

Indeed, the key question to ask of yourself is not what went "wrong" and instead: "What did I do well, even if the outcome wasn't the best?" Practice at asking this question again and again till you get it right, the Gabby Douglas way.

I am not suggesting for a moment that you do not have to have conscience. Or that you should love the uncertainty of waiting things out only to find problems emerging. Lessons learned from commitments that aren't working or didn't work almost always include feeling awful for having created other people's expectations that things would work out great—but didn't.

Nor is it any fun to realize that, after having committed lots of your own time (the only thing on this Earth you cannot replace) to make things happen the right way, they happened the wrong way. Maybe the time you spent was indeed lost. Rare is the situation when your time was totally wasted, though, since at a minimum you are coming away from the experience with valuable lessons learned.

The key point here is that you have so much going for you—your successes even when a commitment fails—even when you are living through the inevitable disappointment of an outcome you didn't want. These successes are rooted in what you did with the best of intentions to make the commitment work and, even if it didn't, in the many resulting opportunities to engineer course corrections for future commitments, and perhaps make amends for past actions that caused others pain.

You can even make those amends when the people you disappointed decide never to talk to you again, simply by doing better by the next people in the next commitment.

If this kind of "practice" moves you closer to "perfection" even though you can never quite get there, there is even better news. Since as human beings we can never reach perfection, then you don't have to worry about being perfect at all.

All that's needed is doing better the next time around than the last time around. Oddly enough, perfection then becomes achievable simply by redefining what perfection is. By this logic, perfection becomes doing the best you can, that is, doing your personal best.

So there we have it. If at first you don't succeed, you are smart and wise to try and try again. Just be kind to yourself every step of the way in the commitments you make. Rather than perfection, your personal best is to do the best you can.

Remember this, too: each time you make it to a commitment's end, whether it has worked or failed, you've acquired special knowledge and experience. Putting that knowledge to good use the next time around will not be the easiest thing you'll ever do. In fact, it will be hard. The payoff is that the next commitment may end up actually working! Each time you try, you will get better at it.

Others will love you for it, too. Especially if they know which *you* you're talking about.

Which *you?* What does that mean?

18. It Matters A Lot Who You Were Then... and Who You Are Now

Exactly!

The coveted word tripping from her rainbow lips
in an enthralling smile of delight.

"Exactly!"

Ringtone of confidence. Hers alone.
Oh to have it brush against me
with its power of delight.

"Exactly!"

A beacon signal.
We have joined hands, hearts.
Hers becomes mine, ours, this lightning nanosecond flash
of humor
        and cleverness
               and perception
                      and rediscovery
                             and intensity.

"Exactly!"

We are Siamese twins.
Conjoined by uninhibited laughter.
Word sex.
Close. Close together. Oh So Close Together.
Harmony.
Stars align.

"Exactly!"

Clifford Brody, June 2005

When we first met, and years later when now we are together each day, it is above all the way she smiles, purses her lips, and drives home just how beautiful and clever she is, inside and out.

"Exactly!" she'll say, to make her point. Exactly.

Who was I then? What did I want that day? What was it that drew me to her that sunny afternoon? Who was I then that I wanted to talk to her, with no idea at all of who she was, how she was or what was behind that riveting smile? I'm not the guy to reach out like this. But she sure was pretty.

Who am I now, so much farther along in years? Some of the changes in what I think now, and how differently I do things now, now after so many more years have passed, leave me almost unknown to myself.

Yet her impact on me every day is as if it were Day One all over again.

Life really *is* good.

Author, left, the little guy, at his oldest brother's bar mitzvah, in 1948. Who was he then? What were his expectations of himself? Of others?

Author, center top, in Paris, in 1970, to his right, the incomparable Nicole Hébert, a genius in all matters marketing. What were his expectations at that luncheon?

The author, top center, not too long ago, with family, including David Klein, right, our "Uncle Buddy". Whatever the author's past expectations, there are fewer of them today...and better ones...

We did not change as we grew older; we just became more clearly ourselves.

Lynn Hall

Because things are the way they are, things will not stay the way they are.

Bertold Brecht

Time is a dressmaker specializing in alterations.

Faith Baldwin

I put a dollar in one of those change machines. Nothing changed.

George Carlin

Why do you go away? So that you can come back. So that you can see the place you came from with new eyes and extra colors. And the people there see you differently, too. Coming back to where you started is not the same as never leaving.

Terry Pratchett, A Hat Full of Sky

"You're always you, and that don't change, and you're always changing, and there's nothing you can do about it."

Neil Gaiman, The Graveyard Book

"Practice makes perfect" is not...

...just a catchphrase when we're talking about commitments. Rather, it is an effective practical guide for identifying the best elements or mistakes of past commitments and using them to increase the odds that today's commitments or tomorrow's will end successfully.

By now, though, if you have made it this far in this book, you'll perhaps have already bemoaned that there sure seems to be a lot of things to memorize about commitments.

The good news is that you may not have to remember as much as you think, not even those nine ingredients and the other benchmarks you have uncovered in these pages, because they are all listed for your convenience at the back of this volume. Once you've seen that list, you'll realize right away how easily you will be able to use that summary as your own personal yardstick for measuring what worked for the commitments marking your life, what didn't, and what's worth remembering for the next time around.

In fact, the only things that are worth memorizing when you make a commitment will be based on *your actual experience*, not the concepts offered up in these pages or in any other book. Your experience will always include events that may or may not have worked out well. Remembering the unhappy parts is a valuable tool to help prevent you from repeating them. Remembering what worked well is equally valuable: how can we not benefit from employing successful techniques the next time around?

Judging what worked and what didn't—and why—requires you to memorize some things about the commitments themselves, or to write them down for future reference. If you have the commitment in writing, of course, it becomes easy to remember what the original commitment was all about. If the commitment is not defined in written words, it will be harder to accurately recall lots of these details, or for Person A and Person B to agree on what they originally committed to do, much less why.

Matters get even more complicated when it is a commitment centered on an intangible goal, like "loving, honoring and cherishing." Remembering what that meant when the commitment was first made is impossibly hard. So is writing it down in the first place, which is why almost no one tries to do it.

Thus, as nice as it sounds when I say that it is good to write these things down, the fact of this being so hard to do leads to this question: what are the top two or three elements in an original commitment that we can write down now for more easily remembering all the rest of them later on? Even better, is there just one that does the trick? The *goal* of the commitment? *Who* was supposed to do what? Or *when* everything was supposed to be done? Or *where?*

Certainly, each of these elements counts, as do all the rest. Believe it or not, though, none of these choices by themselves is remotely close to being the single most important thing to record at commitment time for remembering later on. Even taken together in a bundle, they place a poor second to the one single most important thing for you to memorize now for later on—which is *you yourself* at the moment you seal the deal!

How do you memorize *you?*

Imagine for a moment that you're engaged to your beloved, and the wedding day arrives. The ceremony is beautiful. The food at last night's rehearsal dinner was far better that anyone expected. Your guests are elated right now, eagerly awaiting both bride and groom to "close the deal" with a kiss. You are beaming. Your spouse-to-be looks stunning. The garden setting is perfect, with the deep blue sky, warm sunlight streaming down and Oh, that awesome mountain backdrop! The flowers are imparting the scent of tropical paradise. The music is driving home to each and all just how magical and meaningful it is for you two to be joining as one in this adventure meant to last a lifetime. And then you touch hands, lips and hearts in a commitment to love, honor and cherish one another till death do you part.

Quick! Fast forward to ten or fifteen years later. You've had yet another argument with your spouse, who's not talking to you right now. The kids are fighting with one other again over the computer game, and you've been left on your own to deal with it. The contractor still hasn't finished the upstairs bathroom, and it is in your hands alone to chase him down. You were passed over again for that promotion, and your spouse greeted that news with a question about what you are doing wrong that's blocking it. The checking account is overdrawn—again—and you are now feeling so, so alone and wondering, "Is this what loving, honoring and cherishing was all about?"

Well, right now, you may not be nearly as swept off your feet as you were on your wedding day. Yet even at this moment of crushing tension, you would likely have no trouble remembering the sights, sounds, tastes, smells and especially the touches on that day when you first wed. You certainly won't have any trouble remembering the words you spoke.

Don't believe me? Try this: stop reading for a moment, put the book down, think back to the very hour of your own wedding day when you actually tied the knot (or to an event like it), and see how easily you actually do remember lots more about what happened at that very instant than what you were doing, say, at 11 AM yesterday.

Why is it so easy to reach so far back but not so easy to remember what happened less than 24 hours ago?

Here's why. When you have all five senses firing 100 percent while doing anything, including making a commitment, you are far more likely to remember who you were—and especially what you wanted and expected for the future at that very moment.

Think about it: many more of your senses were firing at full blast at marriage time than when the two of you went to the fifth restaurant or the tenth club while you were dating. That's why it is so easy to remember where and when he (or she!) proposed, and why we cannot ever remember that fifth restaurant or the tenth club, no less what we were doing at 11 AM yesterday.

Psychologists and behavioral specialists often refer to the phenomenon of sensory memory: moments seared into your memory, without much (if any) conscious effort on your part, after one of your five senses has detected an event and transmitted the message to your brain. Without your intentionally doing anything, that memory is lodged somewhere inside your head, and you may be able to recall it five, ten, twenty, or fifty years later. Maybe.

Imagine, though, if the moment were seared into your memory by all five senses firing all at the same time in concert! Whatever it is, it'll be something you are likely to be able to recall in perfect detail throughout your entire life. Just imagine Gabby Douglas on the Olympic stage at the very moment she was receiving her gold medal. Or you at an event you found truly unique and joyous. She, you, whomever: you are all seeing it, hearing it, touching it, smelling it, and even tasting it! And the chances are that you will never forget it!

If it is true, and it is, that the more of your five senses you are using when an important event takes place, the more likely it is that you'll remember every detail later on, how does this relate to commitments? And how does it relate to the idea that the most important thing you have to remember about the original commitment is you?

When you first make a commitment, the more you consciously memorize the sights, sounds, touches, tastes and smells of the moment, the more you will remember who you were at the moment you made the commitment—and, most importantly, *what you wanted and expected would happen after sealing the deal!*

With that memory comes empowerment later on down the road, when you are struggling to decide whether a commitment you made is still worth your time and effort to keep on the rails, change or abandon. Being able to recall who "you" were way back then and what the you of that "back then" originally expected to result from the commitment arms you with immense power to judge whether the "you" of today still sees value in keeping the deal going.

Be on guard! This comparison may require you to admit to yourself or to others that the person you were way back when has profoundly changed during the course of evolving into the person you are today. Your expectations of life, people or circumstance may have altered so much between then and now that the things that counted when you first joined in a commitment don't matter nearly as much now. Or it may be that those things still count 100 percent, but the original commitment no longer seems to be a logical path to achieve the original goal.

The driver in all this is not what the commitment was all about, but rather what *you* were all about then and what *you* are all about now. The news you receive from your memories about who yesterday's you was compared to today's you may be hard for someone else to digest, particularly if that someone else still wants you the way you were, or wants you to stay in a deal when you are thinking: "How unrealistic is *that* given who I am now."

As an example, one could easily argue that Jenny Sanford was willing at wedding time to live with the uncertainty of husband Mark's commitment to monogamy. Her tolerance then was not her tolerance after he went off to Argentina to be with his "soul mate" (to whom he has since become engaged). There was the Jenny Sanford "then" at marriage time, and there was the Jenny Sanford "now" at Argentina time: not the same person at all, and hence no more deal between her and Mark.

In her own autobiography, Jenny Sanford says as much: based on who she was back before her marriage, she could live with the explicit uncertainty of whether fiancé Mark would be faithful. Based on who she had become by 2010, she couldn't. You can bet that she had all five senses going when husband-to-be Mark first told her he wasn't sure he could stay monogamous in marriage; that surely made it easier for her to remember not only who she was then but to understand who she was post-Argentina.

A few paragraphs ago, I spoke of empowerment. Remembering who you were then and who you are now empowers you with an amazing strength: the ability to accurately judge whether a commitment that looks like it is in trouble really is in trouble, and whether you should keep it going or not.

The most important clue you will uncover is whether the gap between who you were then, who you are now, what you expected back then and what you expect now, has become too large. And you get to decide that all on your own.

It takes a great deal of courage to look back at what you truly wanted and what you truly expected, because that will almost always involve an assessment of whether you were realistic in your original expectations of others, not whether other people were honest and forthright in their commitment to you.

And, much like physical therapy to get your muscles working again after a bad accident, nothing less than a full self-analysis of what's changed in you and in your expectations is what counts the most. Once again, if you discover that the gap is too large between who you were then and who you are now, the commitment is in deep trouble, no matter how bitter a pill it is to swallow for you or anyone else in the deal.

Tough as it is to do it—and is it *ever!*—if you take on the challenge smartly, you are sure to make the correct decision about whether a commitment in trouble is worth your time and effort to keep it alive...no matter what anyone else wants or is telling you to do.

COMMITMENTS

19. Self-Commitments and Your Two Selves

There just is not that much time left for me on this earth to waffle anymore. Too many friends of mine have already beat me to the grave.

Too many others are downing dozens of pills each day, or getting another bypass or replacing a knee or hip. Too many cutesy get-well cards are leaving from my mailbox to reach theirs.

And Uncle Buddy, who let his life slip away before my eyes—My God, he was only 19 years older than me when he bit the dust!

Then bam! Suddenly it dawns on me, right then and there: what a great way to lock myself into pulling this off with no way to escape!

******

Eight days before Christmas, 2012. The cursor is blinking on an empty page. The raucous noise in Tryst is soothing as usual. How very odd that the café's mega-decibels always seem to calm me. No more escaping: either I begin now, once and for all, or I stop flattering myself that I will ever pull this off.

I have self-imposed too many starts and stops to ignore this fruitless behavior pattern any more. It is doing too much damage. The time has come for me to bite the bullet and take on the many months of awful, tedious writing and rewriting that lie in store. Or to chuck the idea once and for all and just move on.

Am I now ready to defend myself against the pre-critics who already were too keen to convey that no one in their right mind would ever spend a penny on the book I want to write or, even were it a freebie, spend a minute reading it.

What a vote of confidence! But was anyone really telling me all this? Or was I in just one more self-indulgent conversation alone with myself about an illusory future as "Cliff the Famous Author"? Or was I just flattering myself that putting pen to paper or fingertips to keyboard could be the tiniest bit important to humankind? After all, who would care if I did it or didn't? No one would even know.

"No one has ever explained it to me like that before!" so many others in fact had been telling me. Young and old alike, their reactions had always been the same. "Gee, you should write a book…"

Enter Brody's Rule of Truth: when three people tell you the same thing, there is real truth in there somewhere, so work hard to find it. Why? Because all too often the nominal truth in what they are claiming as "true" just plain isn't the key truth (they could even be purposefully lying, right?). Instead, the most valuable truth may be lying just out of sight, perhaps in their motives for insisting that you follow their advice, or even in an accidental truth they are disclosing without ever knowing it.

"Gee, you should write a book…" The real truth that they were sharing finally is getting through to me: there just is not that much time left for me on this earth to waffle anymore. Too many friends of mine have already beat me to the grave. Too many others are downing dozens of pills each day, or getting another bypass or replacing a knee or hip. Too many cutesy get-well cards are leaving from my mailbox to reach theirs.

And Uncle Buddy, who let his life slip away before my eyes—My God, he was only 19 years older than me when he bit the dust!

Then bam! Suddenly it dawns on me, right then and there: what a great way to lock myself into pulling this off with no way to escape!

Author, left, at center table at Tryst, in Washington, D.C.

Turning to my seatmate, a genius of a graphic artist with whom I often share the center table at Tryst, I look her straight in the eyes, breaking her concentration on the visual magic she is always creating on her laptop.

"Hey, Alina, did I ever mention to you that I was writing a book?"

"No kidding?" was her comeback. "What's it about?"

You have to leave the city of your comfort and go into the wilderness of your intuition. What you'll discover will be wonderful. What you'll discover is yourself.

Alan Alda

All men should strive
to learn before they die
what they are running from,
and to, and why.

James Thurber

There is nothing like returning to a place that remains unchanged to find the ways in which you yourself have altered.

Nelson Mandela

It's a great thing when you realize you still have the ability to surprise yourself. Makes you wonder what else you can do that you've forgotten about.

Alan Ball, American Beauty, 1999

Who you were...

...when you first made a commitment is rarely the person you are now. Measuring that gap, the one between yesterday's you and today's, is the single most important tool for successfully judging whether a commitment you make with others is still worth keeping.

These two points, taken from the last chapter, apply just as much to self-commitments.

In a self-commitment, you yourself are on the receiving end of that trade of equal values we have been talking about. You yourself are trusting you to do what you say. You yourself have the power to disappoint you by not doing what you expect. You yourself have the responsibility in a commitment to do something to deliver the goods, not just make a noble sounding promise. And so on and so on for everything that is part of making and keeping commitments.

Think about how subtle but real this process is in self-commitments. You say to yourself: "I really have to stop smoking this time!" You may not say the words out loud. Indeed, your discussion with yourself is more likely a silent one. What is certain is that you are still having a dialogue within your mind about what you have to do, who has to do it, what the necessary actions are, how great you'll feel (that exchange of values for what you do), and whose trust you have to earn and keep for the commitment to work out the way you want.

You are also taking account of the gap we talked about in the previous chapter: who you were when you first made a self-commitment, who you are now, and what worked for you in previous commitments whether to yourself or to others.

Most of all, you are very much aware in your heart of hearts that if you go about the same tasks the same way as the last time when a commitment failed, you'll get the same results this time around—

results which probably were not what you wanted then or want now. So you end up telling yourself that something's got to change.

This concept of targeting the two yous in any self-commitment— the you who is making the commitment and the you to whom the commitment is being made—is not simply a play on words.

Example? If you decide that you want to see that spectacular 360-degree view from atop Bearfence Mountain in Shenandoah National Park, you have no choice: you must climb the steep, rocky trail to get there. As you evaluate whether you're in good enough shape, or whether there is enough daylight left in the afternoon to get there, take it all in, and get back down before dark, you are evaluating the pros and cons by yourself. You are also debating with a part of yourself who is on the receiving end of your thoughts and who can help you make a wise decision.

This process, your discussion with a supposedly imaginary other self, is not imaginary at all. It is a refined and sophisticated form of role-playing, in which the two roles are played by two companion yous.

It is not possible to become two different people, you say? Physically, perhaps not. Imagine, though, that you have made a commitment to your wife that, by afternoon's end, you'll have finally refinished the deck out back. Off she goes to her day's tasks, and you know she'll be gone for maybe seven hours, more than enough time for you to finish up.

Four or five hours later, there you are putting the last of the water-sealer on. It all looks so good, and you're now having that imaginary conversation with your wife that, in truth, can't possibly unfold until she gets back later that day. Yet you're already saying in response to her "Thank you, Dear, it looks SO good!" and to that big smile you're getting *from* her:

"I'm so pleased that you like it, Sweetheart!"

No matter what else you are thinking at the moment that you "hear" your wife's compliment, "see" her smile, and "speak" your response to her, your wife isn't back yet, so you're "hearing", "seeing", and "speaking" all of this by yourself. Two people in a dialogue. And even though she's not there, no one will ever convince you that your wife isn't real. The most that anyone can say is that she's simply not physically there yet, but no one can deny that you indeed became two people for as long as it took to play out the scene.

Moreover, while you are having this back and forth with your wife who is not there but is there, you are also confirming to yourself that you sure would like a compliment or two for all that work you've done over the past two weekends to get the deck prepped, re-stained, and re-waterproofed. What a great motive for your pretend dialogue! Who doesn't like praise? And in this case, even though you certainly are fishing for compliments, so what? You've earned them and deserve a lot of credit for a job well done!

Avoid confusing motive with process: while your motive may be seeking out praise, the process you are following in this conversation with someone not physically there is a discussion, using great mental prowess, to work out how the future might unfold if you take certain steps between now and the end-point of your commitment.

And that is exactly what making a self-commitment is all about. It is a process that allows you, if you are willing, to slow down enough for taking the best possible account of all that a commitment portends (goals, time, action, trust, etc.), what it will demand of you (flexibility, willingness to change, and so on), and, later on, evaluating whether you successfully defined, acted on and completed the commitment the way you wanted.

"Oh My Gosh!" you may cry out. "I'm left on my own to decide all this?"

Yes and no. You can indeed go solo through the agony of deciding, acting on, completing and judging the outcome of any commitment you make to yourself. No one else ever has to know.

Imagine, though, how different and probably easier the same task might become if you actually chose to clue in someone else.

Earlier in this book, our focus fell on God as witness to someone's vow or oath. The idea was that the person making a vow or oath was working God into the deal as a supplement to his or her own conscience, or even asking God to become a partner who might lend His great global network to help make the commitment a smashing success.

I also noted that one does not need God or even to believe in God, and that people can instead rely on others—friends, authors, colleagues, one's own children—to be witness to the deal or even serve as helpful participants to increase the odds for success.

This idea of working in someone else's help carries over perfectly to a self-commitment. To be sure, at its core, your self-commitment is to and with yourself. Imagine, though, how the challenge changes if you say to a close friend: "Ellie, I've made this commitment to myself to lose 10 pounds over the next two months." Or "Hey, Alina, did I ever tell you I was writing a book?"

Then imagine saying this weeks later: "Ellie, this is going *so* much more slowly than I thought!"

More likely than not, true friend Ellie will ask you a few questions. Maybe she'll talk about how she worked her way through a diet. No matter what she is doing or how, she is helping you!

If misery loves company, don't forget that the company you'd love to have may in fact have a few ideas to help you get past whatever misery is currently in your way—but only if you are willing to ask for that help.

In the chapter about why we would ever make a commitment if they're so complicated, we visited the idea that you have no choice other than to make a commitment if you want to get anything done. Anything. Our focus there even reached to what you have to do, namely meet some other commitment (like paying the electric bill) even if you think you are working by yourself.

The moral of that story applies here as well: other people will always be involved in *any* self-commitment you make, so you might as well invite them in the door!

The key difference, though, between just any run-of-the-mill self-commitment and one that is actually successful is, first, how you make sure that others actually do become involved, and second, whether you choose to let them share in the glory of your actually delivering on the commitment you made with yourself.

Sharing your self-commitment with others does not require a commitment from them at all: you are not agreeing with them to any exchange of values, seeking their trust, or nailing down any of the other things normally associated with commitments.

Instead, by confiding in others about your self-commitment, you are hinting at the possibility, somewhere down the road, that you may run into trouble, and that you may be asking for their advice and guidance even though they are not obliged to help.

A real friend will always help, even if it is only lending a shoulder for you to lean on when the going gets tough. And when that happens, who wouldn't love a "thank you" for lending that shoulder to you.

You'll win twice over by offering it, too, since that "thank you" is also one of the easiest and most powerful ways for you to share your self-commitment success with anyone and everyone who helped you along the way.

That's what good friends are for, right? Well ... almost.

20. What Hurts the Most When Commitments Fail

What I do know is the unwelcome truth that I had made a terrible mistake believing that he would love, honor and respect me in the storybook fashion I had once thought inevitable.

It matters little now—what he did or why he did it to make life difficult for me.

What counted a whole lot more was that in trusting in his love and commitment to me as his dad, I had misplaced my trust. My error, not his.

******

It is never a happy thought for me, what he did. Succumbing even now to these memories as if a masochist fool, I am pulled from too many sides to keep track of how my own flesh and blood came at me so deceptively and with such seemingly malevolent calculation.

No matter that this was so commonplace in other families, including the so many better-known and better-off who are the lifeblood of tabloid headlines and Access Hollywood.

Those are them but this was *us!* Weren't we supposed to be much smarter than that? Hadn't we—hadn't I—done all the right things to insulate ourselves from the corrosive deceit now surfacing within our own four walls? Hadn't we all been on the same page about who loved whom, who trusted whom, who respected whom, and why? Hadn't I succeeded in stoking the singular love and respect that can only exist between father and son?

Apparently not. He seemed to have so cleverly joined forces with my now-ex-wife to help drive the wedge of divorce between us. He even came across as proud of his skills in teaming with others to engineer this crisis and leveraging it for his own gain, whatever that was. Was his eye on the money? Cars? The house?

I will never know, nor am I certain that I ever want to find out.

Only four months had passed, and already he was reaching out with a let-bygones-be-bygones message hard to be believed. Maybe he had been taken by surprise on discovering that his mother's lawyer had so badly miscalculated, that the divorce proceedings would make neither him nor his mom wealthy. Maybe he didn't realize that we would all lose the house, not just me. I don't know what changed him, nor do I care.

What I do know is the unwelcome truth that I had made a mistake believing that my son would love, honor and respect me in the storybook fashion I had once thought inevitable.

It matters little now—what he did or why he did it to make life difficult for me. What counted a whole lot more was that in trusting in his love and commitment to me as his dad, I had misplaced my trust. My error, not his.

I could and would never turn my back on my child, not then, not now. And I do love him. What a special agony it is, though, to live with the sad, somber reality that whatever unquestioned great and good there is in the relationship between this father and his son, there are now big questions of "why" that are never likely to be answered.

How do we best depict that certain special loneliness which is the inevitable companion to the end of a hope and a dream...

How envious I am of people who do not have to be wary of what their parents, siblings, or offspring really mean or really want when they say that they love you.

Maybe he really means it. Maybe I'll find out before much longer that he really does.

Maybe.

When I get logical and I don't trust my instincts—that's when I get in trouble.

Angelina Jolie

You can't connect the dots looking forward; you can only connect them looking backwards. So you have to trust that the dots will somehow connect in your future. You have to trust in something—your gut, destiny, life, karma, whatever. This approach has never let me down, and it has made all the difference in my life.

Steve Jobs

You don't repair that relationship by sitting down and talking about trust or making promises. Actually, what rebuilds it is living it and doing things differently—and I think that is what is going to make the difference.

Patricia Hewitt

It's hard knowing who to trust with your personal life. When you cry in your room at night, you don't always know who to call. So I am very close to my family.

Lady Gaga

So, we have just discovered...

...there is something unique about making a commitment to yourself that argues for letting others know about it, so that they can help you achieve what you want.

What if your self-commitment fails? What if any commitment fails? And what hurts the most when that happens?

Let's say I get to the airport well in advance of my flight's departure for that long ski weekend I've been looking forward to for months! What a great deal I got on the airfare, too! I've reserved my seat, packed my bag the right way—no surcharge when I checked in—and got through security in two minutes flat. I found the Starbucks and made that trade of my dollars for their coffee. I am loving the latte's aroma and how it tastes. I have made it to the gate, the sky is bright blue, and life is good.

Until, that is, the departure board signals the surprise—*Surprise!*—that my flight is cancelled.

On this long four-day holiday weekend, every flight going just about anywhere is surely overbooked. I know even before trying that no amount of cajoling the gate agents or button-pressing on my smart phone is going to produce a way for me to get from here to there.

What bothers me the most about the airline's broken commitment? It was straightforward enough. I committed to pay money—which I did—in exchange for the airline committing to get me to where I wanted to go—which it didn't! I have every right to be mad, sad, disappointed and frustrated.

Keep in mind, though, that the question is not how I feel or how you might feel if you were in my shoes. Nor is it about what I do, how I express my anger, frustration or sadness. Instead, it is this: *what single thing is bothering me the most* as I join with the 73 other people in our assault on the airline counter, all of us angrily waving our now-useless e-tickets as proof that God is really on our side, not the airline's?

The sign we all love to hate, but do we ever focus on the real reason why?

What *is* bothering me the most right now? The now-lost chance to ski on that once-every-ten-years stellar snow pack at the resort? Not meeting up with my friends from other cities whom I haven't seen for years. That sorry feeling that the airline could refund me three times what I paid for the ticket and I'd still be angry over the lost chance to meet up with my pals and ski? Or maybe it is all the time I'm losing right now trying to find another flight when I know in my heart of hearts that I won't find one. And, where the hell are my checked bag and skis?

Or it could be something else. Actually, it *is* something else. To drive home why, let's first change the kind of commitment we're talking about, from one involving a tangible exchange of values—money for transportation—to an intangible one. Our old standby— loving, honoring and cherishing till death do us part—will do just fine.

Let's also say that the time has come when you have concluded for good reason that someone who committed to loving, honoring and cherishing you simply isn't, and that it would be better (if not easy) to end the commitment and go your separate ways.

You certainly might be angry, sad and disappointed, sort of like the way you felt when you were suddenly stuck at the airport with no plane to board.

Unfortunately, with this kind of broken commitment, the love-honor-cherish one, it is that airport letdown, only one hundred times worse. Or a thousand. You trusted a real person whom you knew by name (and lots more) to do what he or she promised but didn't.

That is not quite what happened with the airport letdown. In that case, you trusted unknown people with a bit of your money to get you to where you wanted to go, and they didn't.

Bad as that was, it was nowhere near *this* bad! While there are many letdowns in life that are indeed painful, the pain of misplaced trust in people close to you whom you were counting on for major intangible reward is in a league by itself, and it is the worst. The specter of this special misplaced trust hides in plain sight all the time, but once it emerges, it haunts us as no other mistake can.

Think about it: someone we trusted to deliver such important goods actually doesn't, and what happens? Our misplaced trust suddenly looms so large and so real that it burns our inner core with dark dazzling light, virtually blinding us from seeing anything else. When we're up to our elbows in the muck of this wretched pain, our reaction is usually along the lines of: "I trusted you, you son of a bitch, and you let me down. You're a good-for-nothing bastard!"

As you express that anger, watch out, because you are skating on very thin ice. While the facts may overflow proving that your partner in the deal didn't do what he or she committed to do, believe it or not, that's not what is really at issue here. Instead, what *is* at issue is captured in these seven words:

"You bet on a horse that lost!"[43]

Once again, the most important word in that sentence is "you", and in this case, it is pointing to you yourself rather than any other person as the source of the pain you're feeling,

Think about it. What is *really* bothering you the most at the airport when your flight is cancelled or that love-honor-cherish commitment comes to an end?

It is that you, and no one else except you yourself, were responsible for making a decision to trust someone else who didn't do what he or she committed to do.

There is not a soul alive who does not feel the exquisite agony of misplaced trust at one point or another every day—even many times a day! Sometimes the pain is fleeting. How many times have we trusted the weather reporter's forecast for nice sunny weather, made our plans for an outing, and been disappointed by rain? How many times have the kids been looking forward to that snow day and sledding, which never came despite the Doppler radar and all that other fancy stuff lighting up last night's TV screen?

"Why did I ever believe in them? Why did I ever trust them?" That's what hurts the most.

Sometimes the pain is lasting. How many times have you trusted an elected leader to deliver on a promise only to learn he's been on the take and is now going to jail? How many times have we trusted in religious leaders only to learn they have been stealing money or preying on children? How many times have we trusted our own parents to be supportive only to be witness to their anger or outright intolerance?

"Why did I ever believe in them? Why did I ever trust them?"

The answer to that question is very simple, if not altogether easy to live with. You believed in them, trusted them, and joined with one another in a mutual commitment because there was absolutely no other way to get anything done.

Psychiatrists and psychologists always advise that people should not beat up on themselves as often as they do. That, too, is simple to say, but sometimes hard for people to do. No matter how hard it is, we have to do it once we discover that we have misplaced our trust.

What makes it easier not to beat up on yourself in this situation is this: if you have no other choice than to trust someone else to deliver on a promise, and if no human being is perfect, then your misplaced trust is part of being human, and thus it is inevitable that misplacing your trust is bound to happen from time to time.

Not that the consequences of your misplaced trust are trivial or will always disappear. Instead, accepting that sometimes things just don't work out the way they were intended lessens the time you spend centered on the pain of it all. It also speeds up the process of getting past that agony and taking another risk to trust someone else which—inevitably—you will have to do.

One more thing: when you center on your own role—and misfortune—in placing trust in someone who didn't deliver, you are showing an exceptionally pure form of courage. It takes guts to face a failed commitment head on, but it takes even more guts to figure out how you placed trust in someone who turned out to be undeserving of it. It takes guts to ask yourself: "What could I have done differently then?" Or "What can I do differently now in judging whether I should trust someone else?"

When you ask these questions, you are showing a very special and fabulous strength. How? By writing, in your mind or on paper, the lessons learned from your experience, and how you can profit from them in the future.

There is more. In suggesting that you outline these consequences of misplaced trust, I have *not* said that you need to figure out the "wrong" choice you made by trusting in a person who does not deliver on a commitment or no longer deserves your trust. Nor did I say that you made a "bad" choice, or that you bet on the "wrong" horse.

I am purposefully avoiding words like *right, wrong, good,* and *bad* for a keenly specific reason. Each of those words can so be severely judgmental, especially *wrong* and *bad,* that it is wise and smart to find ways to avoid using them altogether.

To do it, you can simply (and easily!) center solely and squarely on the three factual elements of misplaced trust:

– We made a choice to trust someone who did not do what was expected.

– Our making these choices was an inevitable part of the risks we accepted in being part of any commitment.

– Since no one can predict the future, it is as normal as the sunrise—part of being human—that sometimes the person we choose to trust cannot or will not do what's called for.

If all this is true, then why are we so inclined to say that we "... made a *bad* choice..." or "...bet on the *wrong* horse..."?

The answer lies in those oft-heard and oft-joked-about two-word blandishments: "Bad dog!" or "Bad girl!" or "Bad boy!" Whenever you hear those words, it is surely because someone is criticizing someone else for doing something "wrong". We learn early on that these words are the ones most people normally use to send a scolding message, because they want someone or something to stop doing whatever they are doing and go about things in a different way.

So far, so good. But think about this: in every instance when people shout out these words, they're talking about what they *believe* to be the "right" thing to do or the "good" thing to do. Unfortunately, by definition, what I believe is right may very well not be what you think is right, just like people who vote Republican think they are right and that Democrats aren't. And vice versa.

Who's to say, then, what the real truth is? Who's to say who is really "right" or what is really "right"? Of course you're on solid ground to say: "It is all a matter of opinion!" Of course it is! And that is exactly the point here.

The only "fact" in any judgmental declaration of who or what is right, wrong, good, or bad is this: although the person making that judgment surely believes what she's saying is correct (her alleged "fact"), what she is really saying about who's right or wrong is pure opinion.

Opinion always requires judgment. And, in fact, any statement is completely judgmental about your having bet on the "wrong" horse by trusting someone who may not have deserved it. How different it would be if that same critic said simply that you bet on a horse that lost the race. She would merely be stating a fact (unless the horse actually won and she misread the board!).

The point of all this: forget about nailing the other person, and look askance on anyone trying to nail you for doing anything "wrong"! The best way to lessen the prospect of beating up on yourself for having trusted someone who did not do what he or she said is to choose nonjudgmental words to depict what you factually did. You trusted a person who did not do what was expected. No less than that, but also no more than that!

Arguing whether that person was "bad", or whether you were "wrong" in trusting that person is wholly judgmental—and a waste of precious time that you can never replace.

Why bother with that judgment at all if it will do nothing for you when all is said and done? Especially when avoiding these value judgments makes it easier for us to tolerate and overcome the pain, after a commitment fails, of recognizing that we may have made quite a mistake in trusting someone else, and to figure out a different way of making these choices in the future and upping the chances for success.

To err is human, to forgive divine. This is a very wise maxim handed down to us over centuries. Try it on yourself. We all make mistakes. They are a core part of being human and therefore are inevitable. You can debate forever whether mistakes are bad or good, but it won't take you anywhere useful.

What will get you far is the greater wisdom you now have for judging whether future commitment partners will deliver what they say they will, and making a commitment that is much more likely to succeed than fail.

If you want to get anything done, that is.

21. Where To From Here

Anne-Marie.

Still the slightest wisp of a thing, she was stunningly beautiful, in her early thirties. Like every other woman in France it seemed, she had been magically born with a sense of style and self unmatched anywhere else in the world.

Anne-Marie's dark brown hair was fashionably cut, erotic in the way it lightly caressed her neck and chin when she smiled. My goodness, how that smile had seduced me, drawn me in when we first met! How I had wanted to dive into those mysterious eyes and reach down to the center of her soul, to be warmed by it, to be taken in.

Talk about me being in a world of French-English confusion. I had been convinced that my initial lust for her surely was unrequited. What part of her message now wasn't I believing? What lay hidden within her words, her beguiling allure, the lilt in her tone, the artistry of her tenderness, the stirring curve of her mouth, her lips ... the way her hair so graced the back of her neck...

******

Sitting at the Café Flore, I felt so alone, barred at the gate of the very local community that had once opened its arms wide to take me in, to make me one of the *quartier*,[44] to accept me as one of their own.

And then, suddenly there she was, stepping in silence over to the tiny sidewalk table, more shocked to see me there, I guess, than I had been spotting her crossing the boulevard. Why should I be surprised? After all, this was her hometown, not mine, and she lived only a few streets away, just off Rue Bonaparte.

Café de Flore, Boulevard St Germain Paris 6ᵉ

She belonged here; I didn't. I had quit Paris a year ago. Who was I now other than one more nameless American tourist, an invisible man between countries, a hotel-bound passer-by. No matter that I was on my way to live in Prague. I was Mr. Cellophane here at the café, and the people on this evening's rain-swept Latin Quarter streets could not be blamed for looking right through me.

For most of this unhappy day, I had been up to my elbows in the muck of wretched, self-pitiful yearning, including right now, as I stared up at the balcony of our old sixth-floor walk-up. Ah, how my wife K and I had so smugly looked down at this very café night after night where I was now so rootlessly seated. How we had mocked all the peons lusting in their fleeting, pyrrhic moment of triumph at having found a seat across from Saint Germain Des Prés for sipping espresso.

All *we* had to do was brew our own and watch the same world go by...and then some...from our Latin Quarter perch in the sky. So, so lost in my reverie of those two years that once were, back when K and I had been living the good life of transplant Americans in Paris, that it was only by mere chance that I saw Anne-Marie crossing the Boulevard St Germain before she saw me.

Anne-Marie.

Still the slightest wisp of a thing, she was stunningly beautiful, in her early thirties. Like every other woman in France it seemed, she had been magically born with a sense of style and self unmatched anywhere else in the world.

Anne-Marie's dark brown hair was fashionably cut, erotic in the way it lightly caressed her neck and chin when she smiled. My goodness, how her smile had seduced me, drawn me in when we first met! How I had wanted to dive into those mysterious eyes and reach down to the center of her soul, to be warmed by it, to be taken in.

"Look, think, dream whatever you want," the ambassador had warned diplomatic staff at Embassy Paris, "but don't touch!" I followed his rule to the letter back then, but it did not apply now, not any more. Newly minted as an unattached divorcé simply passing through the City of Light, I wasn't running any risk of a marriage compromised. Or of anything much else, celibate that I was after breaking up with my girlfriend back in D.C. Time to go it alone for a bit, I had decided.

Now, with no warning, there she was. Anne-Marie, coming to sit with me. Wanting to be with me. To talk to me. To hear my voice. So

COMMITMENTS

taken by her delight in finding me there. And there was no question whether she meant what she said. She did.

Talk about being in a world of French-English confusion. I had been convinced that my initial lust for her surely had been unrequited. Earth to Cliff: just how asleep at the wheel had I been? What part of her message now wasn't I believing? What lay hidden within her words, her beguiling allure, the lilt in her tone, the artistry of her tenderness, the stirring curve of her mouth, her lips ... the way her hair so graced the back of her neck...

I didn't have to wait much longer to find out what was in store. After being married for only three years, she unfolded a sordid tale about the too many times Etienne had cheated on her. "The bastard!" she exploded. He had been a serial womanizer. He hadn't loved her at all. "Imagine! Me, Anne-Marie, no more than an expensive watch he could wear to show off the wealth he married into! *My money!*" A saga so new to her, a sorry tale so often told by the rest of humankind since the dawn of society.

I can still remember how much I had wanted to touch her when we first met at the embassy reception. Now? Without any warning, her presence bespoke the grey mold of unwelcome closeness, of smothering intimacy, of cloying words, her hands reaching out to mine across the worn marble surface of a small round table that surely had hosted so many happy lovers...

I did not want to touch her or be touched by her. I just wanted to get away, to break free of her hold, to push back against the jaws of a powerful vise squeezing the life out me.

"I am so sorry, Anne-Marie, so sorry to hear this sad news. I so wish you well, but you will excuse me, I hope, for I must go." Thank God I had already paid the tab.

How my lonely eyes were opened wide in that lonely moment of that lonely evening on my lonely way to Czechoslovakia. How shaken I was to discover for the first time what so many others had already well understood: you can't go back, Cliff, you can't recreate it, you can't live as you did. No one can.

Frank Sinatra sings of being in "the autumn of my years" in his marvelous rendition of *It Was a Very Good Year*. That's where I find myself these days, unreservedly boasting that life has been good to me. Life was good. Life *is* good. I do debate with myself every now and then: what *is* on my bucket list? Where are the places that I must see just one more time before I check out for good?

This debate with myself is sharp, not friendly, framed by the reality that there is no going back to where I was and seeing something a second time as if it were the first. There is no going back for any of us, no matter how much we are captivated by the illusion of our memories.

Yes, memories touch us, shape us, allow us to recall the tentative steps we took along the path of becoming who we are right now.

There in Paris that evening, I learned what it means...and what it takes...to move on rather than trying to recapture the past. Life was moving on, and it was time to move on with it, and to deliver a few special goods I had solely promised myself...solely to myself.

You can't go back home to your family, back home to your childhood, back home to romantic love, back home to a young man's dreams of glory and of fame, back home to exile, to escape to Europe and some foreign land, back home to lyricism, to singing just for singing's sake, back home to aestheticism, to one's youthful idea of 'the artist' and the all-sufficiency of 'art' and 'beauty' and 'love,' back home to the ivory tower, back home to places in the country, to the cottage in Bermuda, away from all the strife and conflict of the world, back home to the father you have lost and have been looking for, back home to someone who can help you, save you, ease the burden for you, back home to the old forms and systems of things which once seemed everlasting but which are changing all the time—back home to the escapes of Time and Memory.

Thomas Wolfe

There is no going back in life. There is no return. No second chance.

Daphne du Maurier

It's no use going back to yesterday, because I was a different person then.

Lewis Carroll, Alice in Wonderland

I don't believe in yesterday, by the way.

John Lennon, Playboy interview, January 1981

Where to from here?

There are many things you might do at this point, but the best recommendation I can offer is something you should not do. Don't make it your life's work to find out all you can about commitments, and don't worry about whether you have remembered enough from all the words in these pages.

For now, let that marvelous miracle machine up there between your ears do its magic. Today, tomorrow, and thereafter, let your mind wander somewhere else than what a commitment is all about.

In fact, don't worry at all if you can't remember this or that detail from these pages. Soon enough, something will happen that will require you to make a commitment. You will be surprised by how much you do remember, or at least how easy it will be to find the right part of this book to rediscover useful pointers to help guide you.

That said, there are some things you might add to your "to do" list that are sure to delight you and at the same time make you much smarter about commitments.

How about some commitment eye candy? Go get that DVD and watch *The Philadelphia Story* or *High Society*, the former if you're also curious about how rapidly American cinema matured in the 1930s, the latter if you love American musical standards, Frank Sinatra, Bing Crosby and Louis Armstrong. Get both if you delight in sophisticated tongue-in-cheek comedy wrapped in sheer entertainment.

Listen to Lieutenant Cable sing "You've Got to Be Taught" in *South Pacific*. Go see the musical if it is being staged in your hometown, or get hold of the DVD. Watching the video, you will have to endure a few scenes where the actual chemistry of early wide-screen movie making in the 1950s resulted in a peculiar pink-orange tint to everything on the screen, but those scenes don't last long and you can use them to shut your eyes and focus on what you're hearing in song and lyrics.

Top: Philadelphia Story stars (left to right) John Howard, Cary Grant, Katharine Hepburn, and Jimmy Stewart. Bottom: High Society stars (left to right) Bing Crosby, Grace Kelly, Frank Sinatra, and the esteemed "Satchmo" himself, Louis Armstrong

Also from the world of music, center on the haunting melody and longing words Natasha Bedingfield musically brings forth in *Soulmate*. Hardly a lighthearted happy tune, Bedingfield's eloquent lyrics point masterfully to an undying truth about commitments: it is so normal to want things to work out the way we planned, and to search hard for another person to help us get there.

There is that mystically enchanting gift from Andrew Lloyd Webber, *The Phantom of the Opera*, particularly the haunting melodic how-to lesson in negotiating commitments offered up in "All I Ask of You." Listen carefully to the words. A melodic love song that always sweeps audiences off their feet, this musical treat also manages to step every listener through the critical bargaining that is required for agreeing to that exchange of equal values you've been reading about here.

If you want more music from The Great White Way, try "What I Did for Love" from *A Chorus Line*, "A Man Doesn't Know" from *Damn Yankees*, or "My Man" sung by Barbra Streisand in *Funny Girl*.

Away from the Broadway stage, there is Billie Holiday's rendition of "The Man I Love," Carol King's own rendition of "Will You Love Me Tomorrow?" or Lady Gaga's "Speechless," not so much the version in her *The Fame Monster* album, but instead the one seen, not just heard, when she sings alone at the piano in the YouTube clip "Lady Gaga - Speechless (Live At The VEVO Launch Event)".

Billie Holiday, a high-voltage talent and a troubled life of her own

Last but not least, there is that black comedy masterpiece directed by Danny DeVito, *War of the Roses*. No matter how keen your appetite for wit and sarcasm, you'll need a strong constitution and maybe a stiff drink to sit through this one. If you come away from the film scratching your head about why they did that to each other, you'll indeed have learned a whole lot about making commitments, breaking them, and then coming back for more.

With all this said, there is a next step you can take right now. Actually, there are two.

First, use a paper clip or the bookmark feature in your e-reader or tablet to mark the checklist pages that follow this chapter. There, you will find a neat summary of the key points in this book and easily follow the logic trail they blaze. You can rejoin that trail whenever the time comes for making a big commitment, or when the time has come for judging whether a commitment already in place needs tweaking or abandoning altogether.

Next, pick one commitment that was really important to you, one that either went exactly the way you wanted and thrilled you, or one that went south and really upset you! Either one will do; you don't need both.

Now, grab pencil and a legal pad. At the top, write down a brief description of what the commitment was. Then, draw a vertical line from top to bottom, dividing the top sheet into two equal sections, left and right, below the summary. The title for the left column is: Things That Worked the Way I Expected. On the right side: Things That Didn't Work the Way I Expected.

Now, list just three things on each side, keeping in mind that even in commitments that failed, some things worked right. The same goes for commitments that worked: some things did not work the way you expected.

Once you have written those three items on each side, put the pad aside for at least twenty-four hours. Then come back, and add just two more things to each side. You'll discover a thing or two about what you really believe, who you were and what you wanted then and now, and you will have begun to perfect the process for planning out your next big commitment.

Five items on each side. That's all it takes.

Last but not least, I'd love to know your thoughts about commitments and what advice you would give.

Let me know: e-mail me whenever you like at author@cliffordbrody.com, visit my author website and blog at www.cliffordbrody.com, and stop by at my Facebook author page: https://www.facebook.com/cliffordbrodyauthor. For any ideas that you would like me to share with others, just say the word, and you will get the credit, not me.

Bottom line: you are always a welcome guest whenever you visit, and I thank you in advance for helping to make me smarter.

COMMITMENTS

Epilogue

After I finished the manuscript for "Commitments" and began preparing it for publication, I met a woman at my "office" at Tryst who was completing her PhD thesis on, of all things, how the homes of famous 19th and 20th century English authors were in fact representations of the writers' inner quest for stability in their lives.

Her conclusion? These authors had embarked on a fool's quest (my words) by looking to their physical homes as an island of stability in the otherwise chaotic world that made up their lives. It was self-deception, the scholar said, because the notion of stability was something that could never be achieved. Why? Because stability itself was pure illusion.

This also meant, she went on, that as an illusion, the idea itself that a person could achieve stability was a lie. Perhaps, she added, it was "a good lie", and that if it was, it was okay to believe in good lies.

"Good Lies". Having stopped me dead in my tracks, those two words left me suddenly asking myself whether commitments themselves were *any* kind of lie.

"Because the risks in making any commitment are so anchored in future unknowns," I asked her, "does that mean commitments are no more than illusions and thus are lies?"

COMMITMENTS

"Sure!" she responded, "and there's nothing wrong with lying to ourselves about it, either."

I'm not sure I agree that an illusion is equivalent to a lie, whether a good lie or a bad one. The definition of lie is a deliberate effort by someone to mislead oneself or others when the perpetrator knows the truth to be different than what he or she is saying it is.

Is that what really happens with commitments? In and of themselves, do they create a false or misleading impression of reality?

It is true that at the moment we make a commitment, we're putting our faith in an estimate of the future that we cannot prove to be correct until it works out the way we intended. Or doesn't.

However, unless the commitment itself is purposefully dishonest, our estimate of its future is neither an illusion nor a lie.

Instead and luckily, it is what it is: an unknown whose outcome we first can estimate and then can actively shape by the words we speak and the actions we take.

That is opportunity, not illusion.

246

Appendix 1: Commitment Checklists

Here are some helpful checklists to help you remember key points from this book.

The key elements of a commitment are...

– goals.

– time.

– actions.

– delivering the goods.

– trusting someone else.

– trading equal values.

– keeping someone else's trust in the deal (and in you).

– knowing that no lifetime commitment will ever last a lifetime without changes.

– being prepared to end a commitment.

Before you make the commitment, you can...

– search out other commitments that seem to be similar to the one you're thinking about.

– ask friends about their experiences and lessons learned from commitments.

– do on-line searches, starting with "famous promises that were broken."

– look to history, music, poetry and other art forms for more examples.

While you are sealing the deal and making the commitment, you should...

– be explicit about the goal, the time involved, the actions to be taken, the goods to be delivered, the exact value of the trade, and how each person will earn and keep one another's trust.

– talk about how you will deal with changes that arise during the life of the commitment, especially if the goal is intangible.

– use as many senses as possible—sight, sound, touch, taste and smell—to record in your own mind who you are and what you hope the outcome will be.

– set up a consensus process for evaluating progress and problems that will arise.

After you make the commitment, you do well by yourself if you...

– use a consensus process to evaluate changes as they occur, when deciding whether to keep a commitment going, change it, or end it.

– ask for help along the way.

– accept equal responsibility for anything that is going wrong, and for taking an active role in any solution meant to keep the commitment on the rails.

– are prepared to be the person who ends the commitment.

– periodically revisit who you were when the commitment was first made; don't let the gap grow so large that you'll lose sight of the person you once were, and those wonderful things you truly wanted back then.

If a commitment fails, take these actions...

– figure out what mistakes you made and the lessons you learned.

– think carefully about who you were when the commitment began and how you have changed to become the person you are now that the commitment has failed.

– avoid criticizing yourself for making a "bad" mistake or doing anything "wrong."

– focus on what you did right, and the courage you showed, by taking on the commitment in the first place and putting your time and energy into making it a success—even if it wasn't.

COMMITMENTS

Appendix 2: What is Behavioral Delivery?

Behavioral Delivery focuses on a simple if almost-always overlooked analysis: given all the options you have, how do you literally *behave* at the very moment you decide how to respond to a challenge—for example, taking on a commitment?

This Behavioral Delivery analysis centers squarely on a person's literal behavior *during* that decision-making process. It does *not* matter who did what afterwards, what the outcome was, or even what the decision was. Nor does it matter whether the result you wanted was the result you got.

Instead, Behavioral Delivery targets that very instant, that very moment of truth, when for whatever reason you *actually decide* that you must make a decision and then *actually do it!* We're really talking here about *two* decisions, aren't we, namely the sequence of deciding to act and then committing to the actual decision itself. And we're also wrapping in the positives in this decision-making process—what you did and *how you did it*—that led to your making up your mind to "do it!".

Think about it. How *did* you behave at that very moment? Weren't you decisive? Of course you were! Making a decision by definition is the act of being decisive. Behavioral Delivery identifies and emphasizes your decisiveness *plus all the other positive things you did leading up to your decision.* Yup! We're talking about accentuating

COMMITMENTS

the positive before rushing to find out what was "wrong" or what went "wrong" as a result of your decision.

There is more. No matter what the issue is, deciding to take action is always a risk-laden process, especially in instances where you only have a few nano-seconds to make up your mind. But risk is not danger. Taking on risk is a thoughtful process, calling for a lot of courage on your part to weigh the pros and cons before accepting risk, something you always do when you make decisions (including decisions to make commitments).

If you end up surprised to learn just how much courage you are showing, so be it. The key issue is understanding in detail what that courage of yours is made of—call them your "courage ingredients" if you like. Doing so, you can use this formula again and again and again to accept the risks that accompany any potential reward, survive the process, and thrive.

Examining your Behavioral Delivery therefore is a way for you to understand a recipe that already exists: how you do what you already do, and how *well* you do it, not how poorly. It doesn't require you to "learn" anything new, or to "change" anything you are doing. Instead, it calls for you only to take apart a simple puzzle—how you did what you did—understand each puzzle piece for what it really shows about your courage, and then put the pieces back together exactly as they were.

Behavioral Delivery also points to "guiltless failure": why you should not feel guilty or mad at yourself for failing to meet a commitment that you wanted (and were trying hard) to fulfill. While there may be room for sadness, sorrow, or whatever else "unhappy" that might have impacted you or others from a commitment that fails, the core act of your deciding to make a good faith effort at meeting a commitment is a separate matter, one full of positives.

And it is a good faith effort that always points to success. Even a commitment's outright failure brings a special success—perhaps not the success you anticipated, but a success nonetheless. You reached for the stars, maybe got there or maybe didn't, but you showed a lot of fortitude whatever the outcome.

And *that* points to how you will get better at it each time you try.

Behavioral Delivery in Greater Depth.

In its simplest form, behavioral delivery refers to how we actually decide to act and then how we act at the moment we actually must take some action, taking fully into account our knowledge of how, in theory, we *should* act in a given set of circumstances.

Focusing on a person's conscious decision-making is intrinsic to understanding the importance of behavioral delivery. It is an analytical process that reaches way beyond the study of people's behavior. It calls for attention not just to an individual's thought processes at decision-making time but also to the value a person *believes* he or she will receive by deciding one way *instead* of another.

This focus, on uncovering the perceived value flowing from an actual decision about to be made, is very, very important, even if (and especially if) the immediate or long-term aftermath of someone's decision ends up *not* being what the person planned, expected, or wanted.

For example, we are taught that as drivers, we must make a full and complete stop at a stop sign. Given what we know, at that last stop sign we just passed, did we actually make a full stop? Or did we eyeball carefully as we rolled through the sign slowly...or perhaps not so slowly? How did we actually decide to deliver on that nominal requirement to stop, what did we then actually do, and what did we perceive as the value in making the choice we did?

Behavioral delivery is all about how, at the moment we must make a choice, we actually decide to do something based on how we believe we're supposed to behave, and the value we believe we will receive as a result of our actual choice.

You'll read more on the value of rolling past that stop sign in just a bit. Right now, let's say you're on a business trip driving a rental car in a country whose language you do not read or understand. Before you left the airport, you asked the attendant for directions to your hotel, which was about an hour's drive south of the airport, just off the main highway.

"Don't worry," she said, "because most of the highway signs are written in English as well as Cyrillic letters, so you'll recognize the exit for the hotel along the way."

About an hour into your drive, you see a big overhead sign that in fact indicates that this is the exit where you're supposed to leave the highway to reach the hotel. Sadly, you don't know it, because the sign is written only in Cyrillic letters, and you don't get the message. Sure, the airport attendant meant well, but she was mistaken in her instructions to you.

So what happens? Based on your actual and precise understanding of how you were supposed to act in a given set of circumstances—you were led to believe that there would be a bi-lingual sign telling you where to exit—you roll right on past the correct exit, missing a critical step in a process to get you from "here" to "there." You did this not just because you couldn't read words written in Cyrillic but also because you thought you knew exactly what to do: look for a sign in English as well as the local language showing your hotel's name.

Your behavioral delivery—deciding to go straight and then actually doing it when you should have exited to the right—was dictated by your understanding of how you should act in a given set of circumstances. And you felt value in making that decision.

Notice that here, we are not talking about fault, mistakes, or any shoulda's, coulda's, or woulda's. Our focus is strictly on behavioral delivery, or what we might call the "did-a's", what we actually decided to do and did, based on what we actually believed we *should* do.

When we look carefully at our behavioral delivery, we will almost always discover that even though we may have been headed in the wrong direction, we may have been doing exactly what we were expected to do. Knowledge that we were doing the correct thing is real power. In my opinion, it is the key built-in asset we all have not only for lightening up on our own self-criticism but also directing others to lighten up on us.

The recipe for that lightening up is hiding in plain sight: focusing first on what we are doing right before drilling down on what we are doing wrong.

Take that stop sign example I described above. If the person who rolled through the stop sign was spotted by a policeman and stopped, if he then explained to the policeman that he was rushing his wife to the hospital because she was about to give birth, and if he then got a police escort to the hospital instead of a traffic citation, what exactly was the true value of the driver's nominal errant behavior when rolling through the stop sign?

Pretty high value, I'd say.

Academics and experts in psychiatry, psychology, and cognitive behavior therapy (CBT) know that part and parcel of their deservedly respected crafts is the essential element of behavioral change: how people should *change* their behavior based on the new knowledge they acquire as a result of their treatment.

There is a lot positive to be said for this approach. Certainly, I would not have been able to lose weight I needed to lose had I not changed my eating habits the way my doctor was advising. In a word, he was insisting, I had to change my behavior. Wouldn't I have been a fool doing anything else!

This said, it is not a given that we always have to change our behavior in order to achieve better results. Quite the contrary: we may be doing a lot of things superbly well and simply not know it. Worse, we may not think it important at all to dissect what we're doing very, very well simply because everyone's assumption is that we're making mistake after mistake...after mistake.

It is said: "If it ain't broke, don't fix it!" The logic of behavioral delivery centers on inventorying and then valuing what you're doing well before acting on the notion that something can be "fixed" only by changing your behavior.

Think about it. Today, the notion is all-pervasive in virtually all forms of counselling that the only way you can prevent repeating a bad outcome is to change your behavior, whether that outcome is a "bad" temper, "bad" drug addiction, "bad" alcoholism, "bad" reckless driving, or "bad" anything else.

The question arises, though, as to what doesn't have to change before centering on what does. Seems simple enough to answer, right? Well, it isn't, because we're not very well trained to do it. To understand why, consider how widely this conventional wisdom is shared among professional therapists regarding the need to get people to change their behavior:

> Cognitive Behavioral Therapy (CBT) is an action-oriented form of psychosocial therapy that *assumes* that maladaptive, or faulty, thinking patterns cause maladaptive behavior and "negative" emotions. (Maladaptive behavior is behavior that is counter-productive or interferes with everyday living.) The treatment focuses on changing an individual's thoughts (cognitive patterns) in order to change his or her behavior and emotional state (italics are mine).

> Theoretically, cognitive-behavioral therapy can be employed in any situation in which there is a pattern of unwanted behavior accompanied by distress and impairment. It is a recommended treatment option for a number of mental disorders, including affective (mood) disorders, personality disorders, social phobia, obsessive-compulsive

disorder (OCD), eating disorders, substance abuse, anxiety or panic disorder, agoraphobia, post-traumatic stress disorder (PTSD), and attention-deficit/hyperactivity disorder (ADHD). It is also frequently used as a tool to deal with chronic pain for patients with illnesses such as rheumatoid arthritis, back problems, and cancer. Patients with sleep disorders may also find cognitive-behavioral therapy a useful treatment for insomnia.

Pioneered by psychologists Aaron Beck and Albert Ellis in the 1960s, cognitive therapy *assumes* that maladaptive behaviors and disturbed mood or emotions are the result of inappropriate or irrational thinking patterns, called automatic thoughts. Instead of reacting to the reality of a situation, an individual reacts to his or her own distorted viewpoint of the situation. For example, a person may conclude that he is "worthless" simply because he failed an exam or did not get a date. Cognitive therapists attempt to make their patients aware of these distorted thinking patterns, or cognitive distortions, and *change* them [a process termed cognitive restructuring] (italics are mine).

Behavioral therapy, or behavior modification, trains individuals to replace undesirable behaviors with healthier behavioral patterns. Unlike psychodynamic therapies, it does not focus on uncovering or understanding the unconscious motivations that may be behind the maladaptive behavior. [45]

If it is true that "Cognitive Behavioral Therapy … *assumes* that maladaptive, or faulty, thinking patterns cause maladaptive behavior and negative emotions," the question arises as to whether cognitive behavioral therapists generally make much of an effort to uncover the hidden value in what people are doing well and to build solutions based on that core foundation rather than simply on changing all those presumed maladaptive thinking patterns.

For example, what if a person who is nominally classified as an obsessive compulsive eater doesn't always gobble up every last crumb within reach? What if he actually chooses, now and then, to pass up that hamburger or dessert pastry? What is going on in the mind of our subject when he makes that conscious decision not to do something? Do we know? Do we ever try to find out?

What of the depressive person who, feeling down and out as she may, still picks herself up, goes to the library, and tutors English as a Second Language students every Tuesday, Wednesday and Friday? What is it within her that gets her on her feet and out the door that we should want to know more about? Most importantly, what does her decision-making say about what she is doing well and can do well in other circumstances, and how can we guide her to recognize her inner strength and value, encouraging her build on it rather than "change"? Do we ever try hard to find out, or do we simply say: "Well, you did it before so you must be able to do it again, so do it again!"?

This lack of analysis of what is working well within us—and especially why—is the driver for the critical distinction I am making by emphasizing behavioral delivery. It leads to the companion concept of "guiltless failure": why we should not feel guilty or mad at ourselves for failing at something we were trying to do—like making and delivering on a commitment, even a big one that lasts for a long, long time but still doesn't work out despite our best efforts.

As I noted in the Preface to "Commitments", while there may be room for sadness, sorrow, or whatever else you want to call it when it comes to the impact on others of a commitment that fails, the core act of making a good faith effort at meeting a commitment is a separate matter. And it points to a lot of good news, so long as we are willing both to look for it and then to read it.

Uncovering that good news requires a careful analysis of what was smart and valuable in our own decision-making and subsequent behavior: our behavioral delivery. Certainly, our spouses, our family, our friends, and our advisors and therapists can help us step carefully and methodically through this process of identifying the value in what we decide to do and did, how we go about doing it and *went* about doing it, what we finally delivered, and how we delivered it.

We will never uncover any of this good news unless we ourselves take the lead first in identifying what we did well and then insisting that others follow our lead in helping us accentuate these positives before jumping on the bandwagon of all the negatives. If we don't insist that the first stop is a thorough inventory of the good news, we ourselves and everyone around us will inevitably opt for doing something much easier: telling us only what we didn't do well and how we need to change.

Even in cases where outcomes are less than happy, we can and should demand—of ourselves and others—to concentrate first on what we were and still are doing well in our behavioral delivery. Defining our behavioral delivery baseline of "things done well", even when the results weren't the best, identifies and preserves valuable elements of our behavior that otherwise will remain forever out of reach.

COMMITMENTS

About the Author

Born and raised in New York City and a long-time resident of Washington, D.C., Clifford Brody has lived the life of an Army officer, U.S. diplomat, C-level business and marketing consultant to multinational companies, entrepreneur, and husband, father, brother, and uncle.

Not all of these jobs, he is quick to admit, worked out quite the way he or anyone else expected. And like many others, he believes, the failures he encountered along the way taught him far more valuable lessons than did any success.

Brody has been spotted in his driveway all too often doting over his two aging BMWs even when it is below freezing outside, probably because they won't start despite his tinkering, or maybe because of it!

These days, he also spends a fair amount of time working with Washington D.C. area not-for-profits to advance their missions in improving water resources, childhood education, and health services for the less fortunate.

COMMITMENTS

Notes

---

[1] I'm referring not just to the idea but also to the logic of the Harold Arlen / Johnny Mercer 1944 popular hit tune: *Ac-Cent-Tchu-Ate the Positive*. More about this later in the book.

[2] CNN Money: http://money.cnn.com/2000/01/10/deals/aol_warner/

[3] New York Times: : How the AOL-Time Warner Merger Went So Wrong", by Jim Arango, January 10, 2010

[4] Eventing (also known as horse trials) is an equestrian event where a single horse and rider combination compete against other combinations across the three disciplines of dressage, cross-country, and show jumping.

[5] In all versions of the Bible save one, 1 Corinthians 7:27 reads along these lines: "Art thou bound unto a wife? Seek not to be loosed. Art thou loosed from a wife? Seek not a wife." (King James Version) or "Are you bound to a wife? Do not seek to be released. Are you released from a wife? Do not seek a wife." (New American Standard Bible). It took until the 1970s for "commitment" to surface inartfully in 1 Corinthians 7:27: "Are you pledged to a woman? Do not seek to be released. Are you free from such a commitment? Do not look for a wife." (New International Version). You be the judge: does that last rendition *really* capture the original intent? As for those of you (including my computer's spellchecker) who hold that "inartful" is not a real word, I can only refer you to William Safire's wonderful column in the July 20, 2008 issue of the New York Times Magazine,

where he wrote: "Inartful means 'awkwardly expressed but not necessarily untrue; impolitic; ill-phrased; inexpedient; clumsy.' Welcome, lexical orphan parented by political usage, to the delights of definition!" Safire's full column, replete with fascinating historical tidbits, is at:
http://www.nytimes.com/2008/07/20/magazine/20wwln-safire-t.html?_r=0.)

[6] Oxford University Press, 1995

[7] Before her marriage to Henry VIII, Catharine had been married just before her 16th birthday to Henry's older brother Arthur. Arthur died in 1502 only five months after their marriage when Henry was only 10 years old. Catharine's eventual marriage to Henry seven years later in mid-1509 was, to say the least, "arranged" by negotiation and treaty agreement between England and Spain. The fact of Catharine's first marriage to Arthur, and her unquestioned standing as widow to the deceased Prince Arthur after the 1533 annulment of her marriage to Henry, assured her status as "Princess Dowager" after the annulment, and she lived out a Spartan existence north of London until her death on January 7, 1536.

[8] You are right if you're thinking that *The Philadelphia Story* sounds awfully like the equally wonderful *High Society*, released by MGM in 1956 and starring the poised and beautiful Grace Kelly plus the marvelous team of cut-ups Bing Crosby, Frank Sinatra, and Louis Armstrong. Haven't see *High Society?* Go on back to the library or the web for that one, too. What a treat!

[9] See this: http://www.businessinsider.com/10-super-successful-co-founders-and-why-their-partnerships-worked-2010-7?op=1

[10] See http://en.wikipedia.org/wiki/Traitorous_eight

[11] On November 15, 2013, National Public Radio's Composers datebook was to broadcast:

"Today's date marks the anniversary of the first performance of Jerome Kern's 'Show Boat,' produced in 1927 at the National Theater in Washington, D.C. by Florenz Ziegfeld.

Show Boat's book and lyrics were by Oscar Hammerstein II, adapted from Edna Ferber's novel, which had been published only the year before. It was a most unusual story for a musical, and dealt frankly with alcoholism and interracial marriage. Mixing tragic and comic elements was something simply unheard of in American musical theater of that time.

Ziegfeld's secretary recalled that before the Washington premiere the great producer fretted that audiences would be disappointed that the girls on stage were wearing much too much clothing for a typical Ziegfeld show. There was little or no applause following the November 15th premiere, and Ziegfeld assumed that Show Boat was a flop. But the Washington audiences were simply too stunned to react.

When Ziegfeld's secretary called to tell his boss that there were long lines waiting to buy tickets for subsequent performances, at first Ziegfeld didn't believe him. But by the time Show Boat opened on Broadway the following month, even the Great Ziegfeld knew he had a hit on his hands—and one based on great music and a powerful book, with nary a scantily-glad show girl in sight!

After Show Boat, the American musical theater would never be the same..." (See: http://composersdatebook.publicradio.org/ and click on the "archive" link)

[12] See: http://en.wikipedia.org/wiki/Oklahoma!

[13] No more eloquent proof of this lies in many of the works of Mark Twain and especially in Margaret Mitchell's astounding literary masterpiece, Gone With The Wind, first published in 1936, and brought to the screen three years later in full color, not black-and-white, through the then-miracle of "high-tech" Technicolor. It is the book, though, not the film, that drives home Kousser's point in jaw-dropping ways that may indeed unsettle you but for certain will leave you much wiser for reading Mitchell's work of genius cover to cover.

[14] in Wikipedia: http://en.wikipedia.org/wiki/Plessy_v._Ferguson

---

[15] About $625 in 2013 dollars

[16] Bishop, David W. "Plessy v. Ferguson: A Reinterpretation." The Journal of Negro History. 62. no. 2 (April 1977): 125-133, as cited (footnote 11) in Wikipedia: http://en.wikipedia.org/wiki/Plessy v. Ferguson

[17] http://en.wikipedia.org/wiki/Plessy v. Ferguson#cite note-14

[18] http://en.wikipedia.org/wiki/Plessy v. Ferguson. Though far from complete in every last detail, Wikipedia's discussion of Plessy v Ferguson includes a very useful summary of what happened next. Take a moment to go on the Web and read it..

[19]   See http://en.wikipedia.org/wiki/Molotov%E2%80%93Ribbentrop Pact

[20] Those quote marks around the word "wrong" are intentional. In Chapter 20, you will uncover why.

[21] From the book *Healing Into Possibility*. Copyright © 2009 by Alison Bonds Shapiro. Reprinted with permission from New World Library/H J Kramer Inc. www.NewWorldLibrary.com.

[22] Yes, Woodro, not Woodrow...and one of the few genuinely kosher delis left in the Greater New York City metro area. So ordinary in the way it looks—no pretense at all, love it!—and so extraordinary in the food it serves. Worth all the time and energy it takes to get there.

[23] That is, Buddy managed to slip in his humor only when the rest of the family wasn't arguing violently over this Democrat, that Republican, who was right or wrong about the Middle East, or how the at-that-moment New York City mayor was a total screw-up.

[24] A seemingly free choice when in fact there is no real alternative or the necessity of accepting one of two or more equally objectionable alternatives. Origin: Thomas Hobson, 1631 English liveryman who required every customer to take the horse nearest the door. First Known Use: 1649. See:

---

http://www.merriam-webster.com/dictionary/hobson's+choice

[25] Yes, I know that if I valued my job and feared that I'd be fired unless I showed up on time, there may have been somewhat of an exchange of values: they wanted me there and I wanted to keep my job, and thus there was "consideration" since we both got what we wanted, right? But no one actually said he'd fire me if I didn't show up on time, and I may have been way off the mark believing I ever was at risk of losing my job by showing up late or not at all. Why this uncertainty? Because there was no two-way "consideration" offered by anyone in exchange for anything, no explicit two-way commitment on anyone's part to do anything, and instead only a bunch of my own and probably erroneous assumptions.

[26] A chain of stop-and-shop gas stations in the mid-Atlantic U.S.

[27] For you attorneys and businesspeople out there, this is the consummate choice you have when writing contracts: either keep it simple or try to write into the document everything that could go wrong and the remedies, too. The former works a whole lot better, in my humble opinion and many smart lawyers.

[28] *America's Golden Girl*, Vanity Fair, October, 2012

[29] Again from that brain-teasing June 20, 2008 William Safire *New York Times Magazine* column: "Artful primarily means 'sly, manipulative, guileful.' Only secondarily does it mean 'skillful' and is not a substitute for artistic. See:
http://www.nytimes.com/2008/07/20/magazine/20wwln-safire-t.html?_r=0

[30] *Staying True*. Jenny Sanford, Ballantine Books (February 5, 2010)

[31] Actually, she still loved him: "I would like to start by saying I love my husband and I believe I have put forth every effort possible to be the best wife I can be during our almost twenty years of marriage." Statement of First Lady Jenny Sanford, Governor's Mansion, June 24, 2009. But did she trust him anymore? Doubtful! Read more at: :
http://www.foxnews.com/politics/2009/06/25/raw-data-statement-

south-carolina-lady-jenny-sanford/#ixzz2Hb2oLBIk

[32] 12 on each of two trailers in tandem, count 'em, 12, plus 14 on the truck pulling them. Do the math: you have to see it to believe it.

[33] Hitler and Nazi Germany also paid a heavy opportunity cost for their belief that the time they bought with the Nazi-Soviet pact would allow them to build up arsenals and sweep their way through the Soviet Union and Western Europe. Alas, it took the Holocaust, the 20 million Soviet lives lost—and catastrophic worldwide human and physical losses during four years of warfare—for Germany (and Japan) to understand that paying this incalculably high opportunity cost for their aggression was a colossal mistake.

[34] Want a few examples that will thrill you as you read through them? *Name of the Rose,* by Umberto Eco, *People of the Book,* by Geraldine Brooks, or *The Swerve,* by Stephen Greenblatt

[35] Johannes Gutenberg, the inventor of moveable type and the printing press as we understand it; see for example: http://www.gutenberg.de/english/index.htm, or this http://en.wikipedia.org/wiki/Johannes_Gutenberg: Gutenberg was the first European to use movable type printing, in around 1439. Among his many contributions to printing are: the invention of a process for mass-producing movable type; the use of oil-based ink; and the use of a wooden printing press similar to the agricultural screw presses of the period. His truly epochal invention was the combination of these elements into a practical system which allowed the mass production of printed books and was economically viable for printers and readers alike. Gutenberg's method for making type is traditionally considered to have included a type metal alloy and a hand mold for casting type. In Renaissance Europe, the arrival of mechanical movable type printing introduced the era of mass communication which permanently altered the structure of society. (Wikipedia)

[36] While "pain" can rightfully be taken to mean physical *and* emotional, my focus is on emotional pain, including the emotional pain resulting from suffering physical, financially, political, or social set-backs. Or even the pain of something as temporary as getting

stuck in traffic and knowing you'll be very late.

[37] *South Pacific.* Lyrics to the song "You've Got To Be Carefully Taught" Rodgers and Hammerstein, 1949

[38] A maxim often attributed to Benjamin Franklin or Albert Einstein, but the concept apparently predates them both. Worth thinking about no matter what its origins.

[39] Until, not too long ago, when I did.

[40] http://en.wikipedia.org/wiki/SS_Andrea_Doria#Resulting_reforms, is a good starting point to read about the real tragedy of these two ships, their crews, their passengers, and their collective fate.

[41] "Physical Training" in Army parlance back in those days, basic "aerobics" in rank-and-file formation ...

[42] Read, reread, and above all listen to the lyrics of *"Will You Love Me Tomorrow"*, written by husband-wife songwriting team Gerry Goffin and Carole King, originally recorded by the Shirelles in 1960 and later sung masterfully by King herself:
http://en.wikipedia.org/wiki/The_Shirelles

[43] Yes, I know that we usually say: "You bet on the wrong horse!" Soon enough, you'll find out *why* I chose the wording I am using here.

[44] French, for "neighborhood, but in reality meaning the local neighborhood where you "belong" and luxuriate in a special form of self-identity and community acceptance.

[45] http://medical-dictionary.thefreedictionary.com/cognitive-behavioral+therapy

* 9 7 8 0 6 1 5 9 9 9 6 0 3 5 *